INSIDE
Afghanistan

INSIDE
Afghanistan

*The American Who Stayed Behind after 9/11
and His Mission of Mercy to a War-Torn People*

BY JOHN WEAVER

W PUBLISHING GROUP™

www.wpublishinggroup.com

*A Division of Thomas Nelson, Inc.
www.ThomasNelson.com*

INSIDE AFGHANISTAN
By John Weaver

Copyright © 2002 by John Weaver. All rights reserved.

Published by the W Publishing Group, a division of Thomas Nelson, Inc.,
P. O. Box 141000, Nashville, Tennessee 37214.

Unless otherwise indicated, Scripture quotations used in this book are
from the New King James Version (NKJV) Copyright © 1982, Thomas
Nelson, Inc., Publishers.

Other Scripture references are from the Holy Bible, New International
Version (NIV). Copyright © 1973, 1978 International Bible Society. Used
by permission of Zondervan Bible Publishers.

ISBN 0-8499-4392-2

Printed in the United States of America
02 03 04 05 06 07 PHX 6 5 4 3 2 1

Dedication

To all who

suffer because of evil acts of terrorism, and to all who've given their lives in the fight against it, from Afghans to Americans.

To all who

purposefully overcome evil with good by practicing the Golden Rule, promoting peace, and passionately living to make the world a better place.

Contents

FOREWORD   IX

ACKNOWLEDGMENTS   XI

INTRODUCTION   XIII

CHAPTER ONE
Three Diabolical Days   1

CHAPTER TWO
The Road to Afghanistan   17

CHAPTER THREE
A Dream Comes True   35

CHAPTER FOUR
A Bend in the Road   51

CHAPTER FIVE
The Camp at Nowabad   69

CHAPTER SIX
Dangerous Duty   85

CHAPTER SEVEN
A Channel of Blessings   101

CHAPTER EIGHT
Bone Weary, Burned Out, but Blessed 115

CHAPTER NINE
Friends under Fire 135

CHAPTER TEN
The Great Dilemma 149

CHAPTER ELEVEN
Invasions 165

CHAPTER TWELVE
It's All about Life 181

MAPS OF AFGHANISTAN 199

CONTACT INFORMATION 201

Foreword

I SAW JOHN WEAVER for the first time in October 2001 on ABC NEWS's *World News Tonight* with Peter Jennings. When John's face appeared on the screen, I knew there was something special about him. I could see it in his eyes, his smile, and his interaction with the Afghan people. Through ABC and CNN news stories, many came to know him as the last active American relief worker in Afghanistan following the 9/11 attacks.

Impressed by this young North Carolinian, I informed my project director about John's activities in northern Afghanistan. Following a meeting with him in Tajikistan, John blazed the trail for Samaritan's Purse to do a distribution of gifts to Afghan children through our children's project, Operation Christmas Child.

In December of 2001, I had the privilege of meeting with John in my office. We shared our mutual vision of spreading God's love by providing aid to hurting people around the world.

To me, John is a modern-day Good Samaritan. He truly models that the greatest in the world is the one who serves, which sometimes means helping the poorest of the poor in very difficult and dangerous settings. Filled with God's love and compassion for people he gladly ministers with all his heart and strength. John is a shining example of following in the footsteps of the Lord Jesus Christ

—Franklin Graham
President, Samaritan's Purse

Acknowledgments

I'M DEEPLY GRATEFUL for the team that worked together to bring this project to fruition, and I'd like to extend the following thanks:

- To the staff of W Publishing Group and the Thomas Nelson sales team. To Debbie Nichols and Mark Sweeney for setting this process in motion and to Greg Daniel for wisely managing it.

- To Neil Wilson and Mary Hollingsworth. Neil spent hours, days, and weeks with my journal, recorded tapes, e-mails, letters, and me personally to produce this manuscript. Then Mary provided the all-important polishing and finishing touches.

- To the "Weaverville Home Team" for providing encouragement since the early '90s. To supporters all around the world, from Asheville to Atlanta, Coats to Columbia, Nashville to Washington, beyond and in between.

- To DARE, based in the UK, for helping me with priorities and placement in Central Asia.

- To SNI/Shelter for Life International, from the faithful staff in Wisconsin to my fellow coworkers in Tajikistan and Afghanistan.

- To my family, especially my mom, who has loved and prayed for me from the beginning. To my sister, Sandi Lynn, who follows this example and also handles my e-mails. And to my grandmother in Washington, D.C., who has been a model of selfless love and who most recently helped me survive when severe malaria knocked me off my feet.

- Most of all, thank you, God of love, for the gift of life. Thanks for second and sometimes seventy-times-seven chances. Thanks for calling and keeping me by your goodness and grace. Thanks for this privilege for truly it is all about you.

Introduction

IN SEPTEMBER 2001 the United States of America and the Islamic State of Afghanistan collided on the potholed road of world events. These two virtual strangers suddenly found themselves bloodied, broken, and bewildered by the violent events that slammed them together. Survivors on both sides are still trying to make sense of the resulting chaos and death. But everyone knows the collision was no accident.

Since September 11, 2001, I've often had the privilege of telling my experiences during the days surrounding the terrorist attacks on New York and Washington. In television interviews, radio talk shows, newspaper and magazine articles, civic and church meetings, I have been asked hundreds of probing questions. You see, I was an American in Afghanistan when three airplanes dove nose first into highly populated buildings in my own country. All but three Americans and Western aid workers went home from Afghanistan shortly after that. I stayed here. And that simple fact sparks the most amazing conversations.

Almost everyone I meet wants to learn about and understand this wild and complicated place called Afghanistan. People say that it helps just to talk to someone who has been here. Their thirst for inside information arises from fear, curiosity, anger, hatred, doubt, and even faith. As someone who loves to teach, I deeply appreciate the chance to help fill in the gaps in their knowledge.

I've learned so many humbling lessons as an American living overseas—lessons we all need to know. For instance, we really do need to work harder at understanding how other people see us. We also need to realize that situations in other parts of the world are usually far more complex than we can understand from the short, often biased, news stories we see on television.

Until September 11, 2001, my first year in Afghanistan was spent living and working among people on one side of a vicious civil war that has raged here since 1996. Many relief and development agencies work on each side of the battle lines. Refugee numbers swell daily. Critical human needs transcend religious and political loyalties. The problem is painfully obvious: People all around us are dying and need help.

Shelter for Life (SFL), the agency I serve with in Afghanistan, is a branch of Shelter Now International (SNI), registered with the United States Agency for International Development (USAID) as a Private Voluntary Organization (PVO). It's a relief and development organization that serves and recruits internationally, operating in various countries around the world, with many of its workers coming from a variety of Christian backgrounds and organizations.

SFL has extensive programs that involve relief and disaster response, emergency distributions and food-for-work projects, construction and rebuilding, and education and training. Our vision is to eliminate the need for shelter for every homeless refugee and forced migrant in the world. We try to do exactly what the Bible instructs us to do in Isaiah 58:7b, where it says we are "to provide the poor wanderer with shelter" (NIV).

Our philosophy of work is based on the biblical principles of acting with compassion for those in need and seeking out those who need help the most. However, we function with very clear guidelines and under the authority of the governments we serve.

Relief and development work involves a specific kind of service in the world. Followers of Jesus Christ who are called to relief and development ministries often find themselves in places that are open to their acts of humanitarian assistance but are hostile to their preaching the gospel. Afghanistan, as an officially Muslim nation, does not normally welcome any group whose primary stated purpose is to proclaim Christianity or any other religion. But Christians who are willing to offer service, or who have a particular needed skill, may be permitted to come. However, we must be willing to operate under laws that don't permit freedom of speech. Those of us who choose to serve in such settings do so with the conviction that what we can *do* speaks more loudly than what we can *say*.

We are trying to meet the needs of destitute people displaced by the present civil war, but those are not our original or only reasons for being here. Other long-standing needs demand our daily attention and God's continual mercy. Catastrophic earthquakes have repeatedly devastated Afghanistan. Years of drought have almost destroyed that region of Central Asia. Decades of war and conflict have demolished homes, mosques, businesses, and schools. Normal life, in almost any sense of the words, has been impossible for a long time.

Through the darkness of the obvious physical and social needs inside Afghanistan, spiritual confusion and hunger for truth cry out. The refugees we help are victims of a religious struggle between two sides, both claiming to rightly represent Islam. Every day I see the chaos that results from attempts to spread and preserve a religious system by force. This principle has historically been proven true—by Jews, Christians (Protestant and Catholic), Muslims, and peoples of other faiths trying to spread their beliefs against the will of their audiences.

I have the priceless privilege of speaking personally about my faith with friends in Afghanistan. They often ask; they are religious, curious, and interested. I also ask my Muslim friends many questions about their faith. Their worldview has much to teach me. I'd be foolish to live among them and not learn about them. I watch them, and they watch me. I listen and learn, but I have made a conscious decision to be a lifelong follower of Jesus, the Messiah. I am in, and hope to stay in, Afghanistan, not to force a message on them, even though I believe that message is vital, but simply to imitate and obey the one I call Master.

Some people I talk to honestly wonder if being in a place like Afghanistan is worth the effort and danger I face. Some question whether it is even possible to make a difference in the face of such incredible needs. Others wonder about the restrictive limitations—laws, war, strange languages and customs, and so few resources. You'll have to judge for yourself as you read these pages. I only hope my story will provide a sense of inspiration and some answers to your questions. As for me, I'm staying with a people I love in a place where I can wholeheartedly serve . . . inside Afghanistan.

Three Diabolical Days

AFGHANISTAN—Where were you on September 11, 2001? No doubt you remember exactly where you were when you heard the news. I was in Afghanistan. When terror began a new chapter in the life of America, my homeland, I was sitting in the lap of "the enemy."

Like most Americans, I got up and went to work that morning. Unlike most Americans, though, I was very aware that terrorism could strike me at any moment. In fact, a terrorist attack had just occurred in the area where I was working. The immediate future looked dismal and uncertain. Before September 11 dawned, I already knew it was going to be an incredibly difficult day.

No matter how lightning-fast news travels electronically, it never catches up with real time. That disastrous Tuesday morning, when four commercial airplanes intentionally plunged into the Twin Towers in New York, the Pentagon in Washington, and a field in Pennsylvania, my 9/11 was almost over. The Afghan time zones put me ahead of the news. My September 11 actually started ten hours before that diabolical day began in New York City. When the sun was rising on New York City, it was already setting on Afghanistan.

Sunday, September 9, 2001:
THE LION IS DEAD

KHVAJEH BAHA OD DIN—To describe September 11 from my catbird seat in Afghanistan, I need to step back two days. Sunday, September 9, began as most other days in a war zone. The war itself hadn't slept at all; so daylight meant the still-living went out to count the now-dead and assess the damage done in darkness. Night drew back her mysterious black covering to reveal a land of haunting beauty. But the lovely face was scarred by blackened rocket craters, bomb-splintered houses, and bullet-riddled bodies. The terrifying nightmare was all too real in the creeping light of day as the earliest call to prayer echoed eerily across the land, rising from both sides of the battle line. That Sunday morning, fewer Afghans remained to roll out their prayer rugs and bow before Allah.

In Khvajeh Baha od Din, right on the border between Afghanistan and Tajikistan, many people stayed awake with the war all night. Warriors and medics had too much work to do to sleep. The town served as the headquarters of General Ahmad Shah Massoud, military leader of the northern territories of Afghanistan. He commanded the forces locked in a life-and-death struggle with the infamous Taliban. Khvajeh Baha od Din is just twelve miles from my house in Dasht-e Qaleh (pronounced "Dusty Color," especially if you're from North Carolina, as I am). The noisy sounds of war had kept me up part of the night too.

No one suspected the two ordinary-looking Arab African journalists who arrived in Khvajeh Baha od Din earlier in the week. They casually joined other journalists waiting for an interview with General Massoud or a guided tour of the front lines. After all, journalists covering the war came and went all the time. Known as "the friend of journalists," General Massoud often granted private interviews to the media to offer stories and exclusive glimpses of the victories, atrocities, and politics of war.

Massoud lived under the intense pressures of being a military leader, but he was a gracious man, who would make time for a civilized cup of tea with journalists. He obviously realized that resisting the Taliban and rescuing his homeland from yet another oppressive power depended in part on getting the story out. Journalists were Massoud's access to the world's ears. They needed him to fill their quotas for stories about Afghanistan's war against the Taliban. And he needed them to awaken the world's attention to the many other crises his devastated country faced: drought, earthquake damage, refugee problems, the effects of previous wars, and the growing threat of Al Qaeda terrorists being trained in camps virtually in his backyard in Afghanistan itself.

General Massoud's hectic schedule of military planning, casualty assessments, and other administrative duties that Sunday included a typical break for a news interview. Tea was served. Then the typical turned tragic.

One of Massoud's visiting journalists focused his camera on his companion and the general as they talked. Moving in closer for the shot, he pressed the shutter button. That was his last conscious act. The world exploded! The expected flash shook the building and turned the general's elegant office into a tomb full of rubble.

The cameraman was blown apart in the explosion. Massoud's furious bodyguard quickly dispatched the cameraman's badly injured partner. And few doubted the instant assessment of the tragedy: Two Taliban or Al Qaeda terrorists, posing as Arab African journalists, had wired a bomb into their camera to carry out the assassination of General Massoud. Unfortunately the suicide bombers succeeded in their wickedly devious plan.

Within hours, confusing stories and conflicting rumors resounded throughout the country and around the world. At first, we heard that General Massoud had been badly injured but would survive. Many Afghans considered Massoud almost untouchable and expected to see him driving down the road the next day, like a murdered television hero who shows up bigger than life on another program. More depressing stories soon followed, indicating that Massoud might actually be dead. A tidal wave of fear and uncertainty swept over the country. Massoud's death might mean the end of resistance against the Taliban.

As the swirling rumor dust began to settle, Massoud's assassination became a horrible, undeniable fact. Although the other commanders of the resistance desperately tried to delay confirmation of their leader's death, for fear of the effects it would have on the people, the truth spread like a prairie fire. And everyone asked the same awful question: What will happen now?

Until his death, Massoud's legendary leadership abilities kept alive the hopes of what the media dubbed the Northern Alliance. He first came to prominence during the 1980s, when the native Afghan people fought against the Russian invasion. Massoud's cunning and effectiveness earned him the nickname "Lion of the Panjshir," referring to a mountainous area north of Kabul that he and his men fiercely defended against the Soviets. Massoud became a leader of the famed Mujahidin guerrilla fighters, who harassed and decimated the Soviet forces until they withdrew from Afghanistan in 1989. Our own U.S. embassy in Kabul closed that same year.

ABANDONED BY THE WORLD

Massoud served in the temporary government that emerged after the fall of the puppet Communist leadership the Soviets had been defending in Afghanistan. The world was eager to recognize the new government led by Burhanuddin Rabbani, but it quickly lost interest in the ongoing needs of Afghanistan when the Russian army pulled out. And now, history was about to repeat itself yet again. Afghanistan, the ancient crossroads of competing cultures and powers, had once again been trampled underfoot and left for dead.

The nation lay in shambles. The political situation showed almost-daily signs of increasing instability. The temporary lull in fighting simply highlighted a host of other overwhelming needs in the country. Over six million refugees were still displaced. Some had escaped to the west into Iran; many others had fled east into Pakistan. Millions more wandered aimlessly in the countryside, just trying to find food and shelter to survive. Refugees who trickled back into their country often found little of their previous lives to reclaim. Conditions were impossible for outsiders to grasp. Practically every major city was destroyed, the countryside lay decimated and desolate, and the people were hungry, homeless, and hopeless. They had been deserted by the world, like orphans left to dig for food scraps in garbage cans of dark alleys.

Afghanistan's war against the Soviets left the country littered with multitudes of dead and wounded, thousands of bombed-out homes, and entire villages wiped out. Basic infrastructure, like bridges, irrigation systems, water supplies, medical services, and road systems were severely disrupted or totally destroyed. Farmlands were sown, not with life-giving crops, but with deadly mines.

The people of Afghanistan had been abandoned. Massoud himself often remarked that he couldn't understand why a rich America, which had supplied so much military equipment to help them resist the Soviet Union, didn't care enough to help them clean up the mess the war they sponsored had created. I've heard those same feelings expressed repeatedly during my time in Afghanistan.

ENTER THE TALIBAN

With the loss of world support, Afghanistan was vulnerable to internal pressures and external enemies. One group with ties inside and outside of Afghanistan became known as the Taliban—a radical

Islamic fundamentalist group led by Mullah Omar. These young religious bandits saw Afghanistan as an ideal place to create what they consider a truly pure Islamic state.

Unfortunately they also had a larger, more insidious scheme in mind. They hoped to make Afghanistan the base from which they could launch a worldwide movement to restore their version of Islam to its rightful place as the correct expression of Allah's authority and power over the earth. That demonic hope is still alive. They are convinced that Allah has called them to eliminate everything and everyone who is not like them or refuses to join them. Even other God-fearing Muslims suffered at the hands of the Taliban, because they are not considered as devoted or pure. Rabbani's fragile government struggled unsuccessfully to handle the pressure.

Bold military moves by the Taliban led to an outbreak of civil war in Afghanistan in the mid-1990s. Rabbani's government didn't have the resources to match the strong support the Taliban received from wealthy Osama bin Laden and other foreign interests.

Main cities like Kandahar and Kabul fell to the Taliban in 1996. Rabbani fled north and reestablished his government in Feyzabad, the capital city in the northernmost state of Badakhshan. General Massoud served then as Rabbani's minister of defense and military leader. The anti-Taliban forces, who retreated northward, eventually became known as the Northern Alliance. These small groups of Afghan soldiers and local commanders rallied around the charismatic and experienced leadership of General Massoud. They held out bravely against the relentless pressure of the Taliban, who were organized, trained, and backed by bin Laden's Al Qaeda network and the Muslim extremists of Pakistan. Outnumbered by their enemies, and largely ignored by those who claimed to be their friends, the Northern Alliance fought a desperate campaign to protect their precious homeland.

In this area of the world, ancient ethnic territories, family feuds, and tribal conflicts or animosities play a much more important role in daily life than nationality or international borders. In fact, most of the national boundaries in Central Asia were established in modern times by outside governments.

The recent conflict in Afghanistan also had a fairly distinct ethnic character. Most of the Northern Alliance forces, for instance, come from Uzbek, Tajik, and Hazara ancestry. Meanwhile the Taliban draws its numbers primarily from Pashtun groups, although it would be unfair to say that even the majority of Pashtuns side with the Taliban. The allies of the Taliban are Al Qaeda—a merciless group led by Osama bin Laden, primarily made up of Arab Islamic fundamentalists, who have come to the misdirected conclusion that barbaric acts of terrorism can somehow make the world a better place. For bin Laden and Al Qaeda, the Taliban are a useful local group, who share their goals and provide locations for training camps. Together they had planned for Afghanistan to serve as a base of operations for their worldwide mission of religious conquest.

By the time I arrived in Afghanistan in September of 2000, the Northern Alliance and the Taliban had fought to an uneasy stalemate. The Taliban already controlled almost 90 percent of the country. The front line followed roughly the course of the River Kotcha, just west of the village of Dasht-e Qaleh. Since my work keeps me in the area around Dasht-e Qaleh, the daily background noises include the distant sounds of rockets, artillery rounds, gunfire, and occasional Taliban aircraft dropping bombs. We are definitely in a war zone. I see the results in lined faces of suffering people every day.

Though I believed God was ultimately in control, during the next hectic months, things rarely made much sense to me. I often became frustrated and angry at seeing so many people hurting day after day because of the war. I gradually realized that my unmerciful thoughts and feelings were an internal warning to me, as were the external evidences of war around me. I realized how easily I could be caught up in evil. How quickly I could wish ill on others. How hard it is to love your enemy when he is trying to kill you and those close to you.

Five years of civil war came to an abrupt climax on September 9. The death of General Massoud meant one of two things: the end of the resistance against the Taliban, or a renewed determination to fight on. None of us knew that events on the other side of the globe would completely transform the situation in Afghanistan in the next few days. At the time, we were busy just trying to cope wisely with a rapidly unfolding scenario. The situation was obviously about to become much worse.

Monday, September 10, 2001:
A RELUCTANT RETREAT

FEYZABAD—Word came to us from the United Nations office in Feyzabad early the morning of September 10 urging all foreign relief workers to gather for an emergency meeting. The agenda was centered around how to prepare for evacuation.

Everyone thought the Northern Alliance was probably about to crumble. Many were fearful that, since the great General Massoud was dead, the Taliban would soon capture the last 10 percent of northeastern Afghanistan, where our Shelter for Life group had been working peacefully since 1998. We all knew that the Taliban would likely first capture Dasht-e Qaleh, because it was next in line. The city was strategic for General Massoud's forces, because it naturally guarded the border crossing between Afghanistan and Tajikistan, through which most of the Northern Alliance's military supplies arrived.

I reluctantly left the Dasht-e Qaleh area and went to Feyzabad. Getting away from the front lines did little to calm my internal struggle, however. I felt bad about leaving suffering people when they needed my help the most. But if the Taliban had taken the area, they would have killed me before asking questions. Of that there is little doubt. The Taliban would not have liked meeting a green-eyed, curly-haired American on a mission of mercy to their sworn enemies. And my innocent, native staff, even though they were Muslims, would suffer and perhaps die.

My real concern was not for myself. I fully trusted in God's protection, and I thought I would have enough warning to leave in a hurry if the front line collapsed. Naturally I didn't want to die, but I had accepted the fact long before that God sometimes allows his servants to suffer and die. I worried, instead, about my Afghan coworkers and local friends.

I also had to consider what the Taliban would do to the refugees we had been helping, if they overran the IDP camps. (IDP stands for Internally Displaced Persons. A person displaced from his home is not technically a refugee as long as he is still in his own country.) We had heard reports of places where village people had been massacred by Taliban fighters simply because they had accepted help from outsiders. But the refugees still needed our assistance.

Things could change, but so far they hadn't. The sounds of warfare were still in the background; they weren't coming closer. My Afghan friends believed, though, that the more intense fighting would soon begin in our area, since it was the last remaining stronghold of the Northern Alliance. After capturing Dasht-e Qaleh on the border, the Taliban would take Khvajeh Baha od Din (Massoud's military base), then Rostaq. Then it would only be a matter of time until they would march up to Feyzabad, the capital of Badakhshan (home of President Rabbani), and capture it.

As I reluctantly drove out of Nowabad, through the mountains of Rostaq and on to Feyzabad, I prayed for our Afghan staff and the thousands of refugees I was leaving behind. I asked for God's divine protection over their lives. I had told them before I left that I intended to return as soon as possible. I planned to inform them by radio of the results of our meeting at the United Nations office.

I arrived in Feyzabad on the evening of the tenth and joined five other SNI/Shelter for Life staff gathered there. We were all the expatriate men and women left in Afghanistan with our organization at that time. We also represented the wonderful mix of backgrounds that serve together in relief and development work. Four of us were Americans, one was Japanese, and the other was British. Our skills included health or nursing, education, nutrition, teacher training, engineering, and computer science. Our individual responsibilities varied from construction management to program administration, running food programs or overseeing distributions to teacher training, health education, development activities, and emergency/disaster response services.

By appointment, rather than by my own choosing, I was the leader of our Shelter for Life team in Northern Afghanistan during those troubled days. I had been in Afghanistan the longest and knew the languages a little better than the others. I was, therefore, our spokesman at the UN meeting the next day. When our staff discussed the situation that evening, we were undecided about what to do. All of us agreed that evacuation might be necessary and wise at some point, but none of us felt that the time of evacuation had come. We decided we should wait, stay here, and continue faithfully helping wherever we could for as long as we could.

The farther away I got from the front lines at Dasht-e Qaleh, the wilder the rumors became. I knew that Feyzabad was well protected because it's nearly surrounded by the awesome ranges of the Hindu Kush. If an attack did come, it would have to come from the west, and we would probably have days, if not weeks, to organize our evacuation. But other factors had to be considered too. So we decided to wait until after the United Nations meeting the next day to make our own final plans.

Tuesday, September 11, 2001:
PRELUDE TO TERROR

FEYZABAD—On the morning of September 11, I contacted our national staff in Dasht-e Qaleh for an up-to-date report. The Taliban hadn't launched an offensive yet, and the front lines of the Northern Alliance were still holding. I remember thinking that perhaps General Massoud was actually alive, or maybe he had left some plan of action in the case of his death.

As I walked through the oppressive heat and fogging dust to the United Nations compound, the air felt heavy with uncertainty and nervousness. I could see it etched in the worried faces of unarmed doorkeepers at the UN buildings. After we greeted each other in Dari (the Afghan language derived from Farsi or Persian), they were full of questions. These men had become my friends over the past months as I frequently visited the UN offices to arrange details of our wheat distributions and food-for-work programs. They knew I had come from the front lines and were anxious to confirm any of the rumors they had heard. It was hard for them to believe I had been in Dasht-e Qaleh just the day before and nothing had changed there. I was touched by their sincere concerns for me, because if things turned out as badly as they feared, these simple, warmhearted, caring men had little hope themselves. They had pinned their expectations of freedom from the tyranny of the Taliban on the abilities of General Massoud. Without him, they doubted that anyone could defeat the Taliban and Al Qaeda.

The last few decades have taught the United Nations some painful lessons about safety. Massacred peacekeepers and recurring nightmares over members of their staff held as hostages in various conflicts have forced the UN to err on the side of caution when situations become unstable. The real questions quickly became these: How unstable *is* the situation, really? Is a possible Taliban takeover imminent? Is staying here a real security risk?

The meeting I attended included about fifteen representatives from non-governmental organizations (NGOs) working in Northern Afghanistan. At least five of them were my fellow non-Afghans. In many ways, this conversation was like an instant replay of the discussion our own SFL staff had shared the night before, with one important difference. These were mostly hired humanitarian workers, and their discussion of safety was strictly pragmatic. There was no room in their conversation for God's role in the events unfolding around us.

The dividing line in the meeting cut between those who were ready to declare the struggle against the Taliban finished and those who held out hope that the Northern Alliance would use General Massoud's death as a rallying cry to continue their resistance. I also heard several older, wiser voices suggest what I had been hoping. Since Massoud lived under the constant threat of death for years, he had probably left orders for his own replacement. So, it appeared to me at the time that there were more reasons to stay a while longer than to quickly evacuate to what seemed to be a safer place.

One underlying theme in the meeting was the need for a clear evacuation plan. In my simple North Carolinian mind, only two options were clear. Feyzabad had an airstrip that remained in use, and the UN had access to several airplanes. Plan A involved all of us getting on planes, if possible, and flying north to Tajikistan or east to Pakistan. That plan depended mostly on the weather and the air security over Afghanistan. Plan B required driving further east to the only available border crossing at Eshkashem, which would take us into Tajikistan. I became frustrated that the meeting dragged on and on about the evacuation plan when it was obvious that we had only two real options. I suspected that some people, out of unspoken fears, were simply trying to rationalize an immediate evacuation.

Several of us continued to insist that it was too early to evacuate. The Taliban were not moving. Even if they did move forward, the Northern Alliance had typically dug in and become more fierce when their backs were against the wall. So the Taliban would at least be delayed.

One person reminded us that Feyzabad itself has throughout history seldom been taken by force. The city is so well protected by mountains that it can be effectively defended. The city has only surrendered to superior forces after a long siege or after negotiations. But when it comes to battle, Afghans stand and fight. For a year, I had lived close to the front lines, and the discussion of evacuation had come up almost weekly. As I listened to this discussion, it wasn't that I was feeling bold or fearless. I just didn't agree that we were in the kind of danger people were describing.

When I had agreed to stay in Dasht-e Qaleh a year before, we had devised a simple, rough-and-ready evacuation plan. If the front lines broke, I would leave. My first way of escape was only a few miles away at the Dasht-e Qaleh border and into Tajikistan. After twelve months, I had become used to uncertainty and rumors. The more I had become part of the local culture, the more I had come to expect that if I really needed to leave, I would know, and God would provide a way. I would escape *inshallah* (God willing), as my Muslim friends say.

Now I was sitting in a meeting *a hundred miles* behind the front lines, wondering why I should feel less safe than I felt only a few miles behind the front lines. The people I was there to help couldn't evacuate. Should we run from danger when our leaving might actually make things worse for those in need? Why should I evacuate before it was necessary? I was convinced we were jumping the gun, but I also understood that the UN had strict security standards that its staff was just trying to follow.

When the meeting ended, it was clear that the evacuation plan was in place—an airlift by the UN. No timetable was established for when that would occur. Evacuation might come as early as the next day, but word would come to us from the UN if that were the case. The meeting ended around five o'clock in the evening,

Afghanistan time, which meant that it was about seven o'clock that same morning in New York City. The day of terror was dawning in America.

THE DAWN OF DISASTER

NEW YORK/WASHINGTON D.C.—I met with the rest of our team for dinner at the Shelter for Life office in Feyzabad. I filled them in on the UN meeting while we ate. In the context of that conversation, we prayed for God's wisdom and for the protection of the Afghan people. We were deeply concerned about the innocent victims who would suffer if the fighting intensified. We wondered what God was doing.

About eight o'clock that night our radio crackled to life with an incoming call. One of our staff from Dushanbe, Tajikistan, was calling with the first reports of something horrific happening in the United States. We quickly switched to our shortwave radio and scanned the broadcasts of large stations like CNN, BBC, and Voice of America. The news filled us with terrifying questions and over-whelming heartache.

The frequent news summaries quickly became repetitions of the same mind-chilling facts: First one, then two, then three large, commercial planes had intentionally crashed into highly populated buildings in New York and Washington. A fourth commercial plane was also feared down in Pennsylvania. First estimates suggested that tens of thousands of innocent Americans had been killed.

Shortly after we joined the worldwide audience glued to tele-visions and radios, watching and listening intently as the surreal turned real, we heard that the first tower in New York had just collapsed. Without the shocking images that so many were able to see on television, we had difficulty even comprehending what was happening. But the underlying evil seemed remarkably familiar. We couldn't help but think that the assassination of General Massoud and the possible imminent collapse of Afghanistan were somehow part of a diabolical scheme that had just been unleashed on the rest of the unsuspecting world.

We listened, wept, prayed, and talked in an exhausting cycle far into the night, until the news reports became endless echoes of the same sad story over and over. I finally withdrew to another room for some quiet. Of course, I wondered if and how these terrible developments might affect our decision to stay in or leave Afghanistan. I tried to apply the faces and stories of the refugees, who had been my neighbors for the last year, to the people in my own country, but I couldn't. How could something like this happen in the States? And why? Why had so many innocent people been called to suffer at the hands of cruel, evil terrorists? What could happen next?

Exhausted by tension and tears, I drifted into restless sleep. I remember mentally reviewing the decade-long journey that had brought me so far from home to this mysterious place where I felt I now belonged.

My homeland was under vicious attack, and I longed to be there to help the hurting. I also thought about the need for people in Northern Afghanistan to continue receiving food, shelter, and other forms of hope from around the world. God has provided generously to some peoples so that they, in turn, can be generous with others. I simply serve as a channel for that help.

I believe I was sent here to distribute God's blessings. I know, deep in my heart, that I am privileged to be where I am—right where God wants me to be. In light of world events, is there really a better or safer place in the world than inside Afghanistan?

The Road to Afghanistan

MY MOTHER ISN'T SURPRISED that her third-born son ended up in a place like Afghanistan. She tells me I was so eager to explore the world that she almost had to deliver me in the hospital elevator in Washington, D.C. I guess I've always wanted to "go where no one has gone before."

Raised in northern Virginia by busy parents in the seventies, my brothers and I thrived in both good and bad ways under the unfortunate lack of adult supervision at home. By my freshman year in high school, my life was fraught with rebellion and trouble. My decent school grades covered my confusion and self-destructive behavior, but I knew more about alcohol and drugs from personal experience than I should have.

My older brothers deeply influenced my early life. By a series of minor miracles, we all survived to love each other as adults, but we got into as much trouble as we could without accumulating a criminal record. The only upside to those rebellious days is that along the way I developed survival instincts and attitudes that have kept me alive more than once in Central Asia.

I sauntered into adolescence as an adventuresome and independent spirit, who thought he had life under control. I had no idea where I was headed, but I was on my solitary way. Then Tyler, a fellow high school classmate, offered me the gift of real friend-ship. He helped eliminate my false sense of independence. As my first companion who didn't encourage activities and habits that complicated my life even more, he quickly made me realize that his life had some enviable qualities that mine was missing, even though I couldn't name those traits specifically. Now I realize those admirable traits were peace and hope. To him life made sense. He lived freely but not as if he was his own master. As guys, naturally, we didn't talk about these things, but they made a lasting impres-sion on me anyway.

TURNING POINT

In September of 1984, Tyler invited me to a Billy Graham Evangelistic Association meeting being held in the gym of our school. My mother and I went together. Ralph Bell, one of Dr. Graham's team, spoke. He gave a simple explanation of these words of Jesus Christ: *"For God so loved the world that He gave His only begotten Son, that whoever believes in Him should not perish but have everlasting life"* (John 3:16, NKJV). I still find it hard to explain, but I heard about God in a new way that evening. Until that point, my belief in God consisted of a reluctant admission of His existence. Growing up in a culture that considers God emphatically optional made it easy for me to ignore personal involvement with the divine.

When I reflect on my life condition at that time, I'm shocked at my casual ambivalence toward God. Here in Afghanistan, I see similar young men already deeply immersed in Islam. Many have committed the Koran to memory, though it's written in a language they don't even speak. They often share the same lack of personal understanding of God that I had at their age, but they treat their religion very seriously. Their culture makes "submission to Allah" an emphatic requirement. In the rhythm of their lives, the daily, fivefold acknowledgment of Allah in prayer beats perfect time and keeps their lives in step, like a metronome.

Tyler's magnetic life and his invitation to the meeting made a critical difference for me. I still had a long way to go, but an awareness of God began to change the erratic rhythm of my own life. That night I received an offer that was too good to refuse. It appealed to my adventuresome spirit. Instead of an opportunity to experience the familiar cheap thrills of sin, I was invited to join an amazing adventure in life at its fullest. A door seemed to swing open between God and me, and I couldn't think of a good reason not to walk through it. I didn't really know what was on the other side, but my inquisitive mind wanted to find out.

My remaining years of high school and first year of college showed little spiritual growth. I endured my share of adolescent confusion and guilt. But I knew there were two ways of living, and I still wasn't living the way I really wanted.

During that time, my parents divorced, and my resentment toward my father ran deep. I felt abandoned and betrayed, because I suddenly found myself, with mixed emotions, as the man of the house. My older brothers were grown and gone, and before the divorce, my parents had added two little sisters to the family, one still in diapers. I hurt for my mother having to raise my little sisters by herself.

THE SECOND MILESTONE

My original education plan, therefore, included Campbell University in Buies Creek, North Carolina, so that I could live at home and care for my mom and little sisters. In November of 1988, however, I attended a conference that became another spiritual milestone for me. The speaker had lived for years in Uruguay. He had been to the kinds of places and seen the kinds of things that fascinated me. He kept me spellbound with intriguing stories of what happens in a community when people first understand and respond to the good news of Jesus Christ. He described personal changes in people who, in turn, eventually transformed whole communities in exciting and wonderful ways. He brought the lives and needs of real people into clearer view for me.

That night had a profound and unexpected emotional and spiritual impact on me. The speaker's words caused me begrudgingly to drag my eyes away from my own immediate imperfect circumstances and actually to see the sad and hurting world for the first time. Those compelling stories flipped a switch in my heart, and suddenly, even that part of me that longs to explore strange new frontiers fell silent and still. I knew so little; yet I sat stunned before the vast global need I suddenly saw.

At that moment, my personal problems sank to comparative insignificance. Previously blind and deaf to the world's problems, I was suddenly healed, and the heart-wrenching cries of the lost and dying world brought tears to my eyes. I clamped my hands over my eyes and ears, trying to shut out the overwhelming sights and sounds bombarding my mind from every corner of the globe. My personal strength and resources were no match for what I saw and heard. Yet, in that moment, I sensed that I was being invited to join God in His work in the world. I knew I couldn't do everything, but perhaps, with God's help, I could make a difference doing something, somewhere. I had no idea where that somewhere was, and the possibilities suddenly seemed endless.

LEARNING TO SERVE

Shortly after that conference, I decided to switch schools. Since I had surrendered my life to serve God, I wanted to deepen my understanding of His Word, the Bible. I also wanted to know how best to join God in His global work. So, after some careful research,

I arrived in Nashville, Tennessee, at the Free Will Baptist Bible College in January of 1989.

For the next few years, I immersed myself in the study of the Bible and worked hard to sharpen my worldview, like stainless steel against iron. Several of my professors had extensive experience in overseas work, and they definitely encouraged my adventurous attitude. My relationship with them convinced me that, if I was going to live and work anywhere else in the world, I needed cross-cultural training. They helped me understand that when I, as an American, move to another culture, much of my own culture that I instinctively take with me is of little or no value to my new friends. They have equivalents in their own cultures. So the better I understand their culture, the more likely I will be able to communicate those things worth sharing.

One visiting speaker in a worship service made this point very clear to me. He came to the podium in full Arab garb. Stepping to the microphone, he eyed us for several moments; then he began speaking a flowing stream of deep, melodious language. It was so resonant and beautiful, I wasn't sure if he was speaking or singing. Later I learned that he was speaking Arabic. The tones in his words seemed to pluck a tight string in my heart, and I felt myself vibrating as he spoke. I desperately wanted to understand what he said and how I felt. In Afghanistan today, I often get those same feelings again when I hear my friends speak or pray. But now I understand much better what they mean.

The speaker stopped for a moment and then addressed us in English. I expected an interesting message about the Islamic religion. Instead he spoke to us forcefully as a Muslim. He pointed out the inconsistencies and hypocrisy that we Christians unintentionally show others. In that way, he demonstrated that Muslims have valid complaints about Christians.

"Frankly," he concluded, "we Christians are often lousy examples to the world of what we say we believe."

I left that auditorium carrying a sense of challenge that I didn't know how to resolve.

The college also brought in speakers from various Christian agencies that shared firsthand accounts of various opportunities for service. Those involved in cross-cultural ministries connected with my awakening awareness that I might be of some use to God. These agencies emphasized language learning, cultural adaptation, community development, and sharing God's Word in relevant ways. Guest speakers illustrated their talks with exciting stories of Bible translation and the effects of God's Word in cultures whose languages have never been written down. People around me shuddered at the descriptions of primitive living conditions, pioneer settings, and lonely work. Meanwhile, those descriptions whispered adventure and purposeful living to me.

LOVE IN ANY LANGUAGE

On one memorable occasion, a visiting member of Wycliffe Bible Translators did a "monolingual demonstration" with a Japanese student who was attending the school. This kind of demonstration shows how someone who speaks one language begins to learn another language when there is no translator or interpreter present. The student was instructed to only use Japanese, and the translator used an unfamiliar tribal language. He demonstrated listening skills and phonetic writing techniques, along with pointing, mimicking, and showing objects or actions that provoked responses from the student. He immediately recorded those responses on the blackboard. Moments later he returned to the board and read aloud what he had written phonetically. He sounded Japanese! The Japanese girl giggled and broke character.

"You said it right!" she exclaimed in English.

The translator ran to the board and scribbled her expression in linguistic notation, recording her expression as one long word—

"iusediturait"—complete with accent notations and giggle sounds. We laughed as we realized that writing down an unknown language begins without knowing whether the speaker is using single words or sentences. The process was hilarious, but the results caught my attention. Even an exotic language like Japanese could be learned, if someone were willing to take on the challenge. During the question-and-answer period following the presentation, the translator made it clear that responding to the challenge also required training. The possibilities intrigued me.

The speaker concluded by inviting us all to quote John 3:16. I could hardly say those familiar phrases without choking up. I remembered how much those words had transformed my life in September 1984. "For God so loved the world . . ." We recited those lovely words in unison.

Then he held up a huge blank poster and said, "Now, would you please read aloud what's written here."

After a moment of curious, dead silence as we stared at that empty surface, he said, "This is John 3:16 in about three thousand languages spoken in the world today."

The silence dissolved into sadness. The translator's statement stunned and broke me. I couldn't get over the hopelessness that empty poster represented. With tears rolling down my face, I prayed, "Lord, whatever you want me to do, I'll do. If you can use me to do something about this, here am I, send me."

That empty poster was a life-changing message for me. People who wonder why I'm in Afghanistan often ask about a sense of calling on my life. Some even ask me if I heard God speaking audibly or just felt drawn to serve. I can honestly respond, "Well, I didn't hear a voice or see some writing on the wall—in fact, what I saw was no writing at all where there should have been, and that was my call." In ways I am still discovering, God has given me the privilege to serve Him by filling in blank spaces in people's lives.

On the road to opportunities overseas, I had many wonderful experiences serving in various stateside ministries. People often told me I was destined to be a preacher. I love proclaiming God's Word from the pulpit but I knew my life's calling involved more than that. Yes, I realize the people in my own country have many needs, but I am driven to the empty spaces. When I thought about serving in the U.S., I pictured a vast assortment of needs faced by an amazing variety of resources to meet them. Once I began to see the desperate requirements of the larger world, I saw that service in my country might be crowded work. I love the frontiers of service where the challenges are so obvious.

CROSS-CULTURAL TRAINING

During college I also experienced my first personal attempts at cross-cultural communication. Thousands of Kurdish families—exiles from Iraq as a result of the Gulf War—arrived for resettlement in the United States. A number of churches in the Nashville area geared up to welcome those refugees. I volunteered for the various agencies that were involved in this resettlement project—World Relief, Catholic Charities, and Servant Group International. They matched individual volunteers with Kurdish families. We had various practical duties: driving lessons, English classes and conversational practice, helping them find jobs, and grocery shopping.

I adopted Mohammed and his family, and they adopted me. In the process of giving them specific assistance in settling into American culture, I also got to practice some of the principles that I was learning in school, such as working on a new language and the challenges of sharing my life with a family whose worldview was very different than mine. I participated in cultural picnics and other gatherings, and they literally pulled me into their dances and welcomed me at their tables. My Kurdish family took great delight in dressing me for those occasions (so I wouldn't feel out of place). They introduced me to Middle Eastern culture, the practices of the Muslim faith, and the whole idea of refugee ministry.

One day at the grocery store, Mohammed was practicing the names of various products stacked on the shelves. He continually exclaimed over the abundance and number of bewildering choices, but he was eager to learn. As we walked and talked, Mohammed held my hand. Of course, I glanced around to make certain no one was watching. Even though his gesture made me feel uncomfortable at the time, I learned that in his part of the world, men or women often hold hands in public as a sign of pure friendship. So I learned some important lessons about Middle Eastern/Central Asian culture in aisle seven of the grocery store that day.

The work of building bridges of integrity and friendship that might allow me to share the good news of Jesus strongly attracted me. The possibility of working with Muslims strongly appealed to me, like an invitation to travel in an uncharted and largely unexplored frontier where I could serve God. In the meantime, God brought the world to Nashville, and I eagerly learned as much as possible. At this point, the idea of going to Afghanistan had not yet come to me.

Meanwhile I avidly explored other avenues for cross-cultural training. This pursuit eventually led me to the Summer Institute of Linguistics (SIL) in Dallas, Texas, connected with the University of Texas Graduate School in Arlington, Texas (UTA). I studied linguistics and anthropology there from January 1994 until May 1995. At UTA I also found a community of Kurdish refugees, an Arabic-speaking Christian fellowship, and thousands of international students. At the time, at least sixty-five different languages flourished on the UTA campus. My fascination and delight with language learning flamed into passion.

GETTING TO KNOW "STAN"

While at SIL in Dallas, I discovered Central Asia—the vast area that stretches from Turkey to China and encompasses all the countries with "stan" in their names. "Stan" simply means "land." So Afghan*stan* means, "land of the Afghans." I had the privilege of meeting students from several of these countries while studying at UTA.

The Soviet Union had just collapsed, and the "stans" were stepping out of the shadows and into the twentieth century. Many of the "stans" were suddenly open to outsiders: Kazakhstan, Kyrgyzstan, Tajikistan, Turkmenistan, and Uzbekistan. Even countries like Afghanistan, Pakistan, and Turkey, which were not in the Soviet bloc, gained new attention from the rest of the world.

All these countries included groups of people who had little exposure to the outside world. Dozens of languages spoken in the area had never been analyzed or given written form. Even though the Islamic nature of these countries presented significant limitations and obstacles, the obvious needs offered almost unlimited opportunities for service. In the area of language alone, surveys were needed to find out exactly how many languages existed and how they were related, population counts, assessments of levels of literacy, and dozens of other cultural knowledge gaps to fill about those Central Asian peoples.

Over these countries loomed a dark cloud of humanitarian needs. Independence from Soviet control simply turned the internal crises into international problems. Wars and natural disasters continued to take their toll. The doorways to these lands were open to those willing to take some risk in the name of service to others.

I could think of no reason why I shouldn't pursue these opportunities. Accepted as a member-in-training at SIL, I met others who were pursuing service opportunities in Central Asia. We met every day to discuss and pray for these nations. I was interested in all of Central Asia, but I was particularly drawn to Afghanistan. It was a wild and desperate place worthy of my best efforts.

SIL began making contacts to pave the way for some of us to enter Central Asia after our training. We planned to catalogue the various dialects and languages spoken in the area. That study would require extensive travel and wonderful adventures. All the frontier characteristics of those lands called out to me. The more I learned about the needs in Afghanistan, the more I wanted to be there.

INTO THE FIELD

In January of 1997, I flew to the Philippines for an SIL practical field course. The courses in Dallas focused on the academic side of language work; this experience was designed to expose us to the practical aspects of living in other cultures. Four of us from Dallas joined twenty-five other participants in the field course. We stayed in the Philippines three months. During that time, we began intense, supervised, on-the-job training in such areas as introductory language learning, culture adaptation, and conducting community development projects. We received continuous performance evaluations. Every aspect of our lives was scrutinized to prepare us for the rigors of living under the microscope of another culture.

Before our training ended, we went to the Catholic Retreat Center in Bagio City for some time alone and to rest. The grounds were covered with the indescribable beauty of lush greenery and colorful gardens, which encouraged peace and silence. As I strolled a pathway on my first day there, I told God, "Oh, Father, thank you for this time of quietness. I really want to be attentive during these days, so I'm going to fast from normal meals and spend the extra time with you."

Fasting stretches time. It slows down busy people. I didn't have an agenda for my fast; so the first days included a lot of sleep. My body settled into a personal pace. I walked, thought, prayed, and slept. I kept a journal of my thoughts and feelings. By rereading them, I revisited ideas about God that I had experienced early in the week and found them now clearer in my mind. I prayed about Central Asia, aware that war had once again broken out in Afghanistan. We had discussed the rise of the Taliban as a potential complication for our plans to go to that part of the world.

Seven days into my fast I had a dream or vision as I sat quietly in the afternoon. I saw myself serving among the wounded and weary in Afghanistan. I didn't see an identifiable landmark or hear a divine voice, but I sensed that I was among Afghan people. In fact, the most memorable aspect of the dream was the painful clarity of what I watched myself doing—helping the poor. I don't remember at what point I stopped *seeing* and started *thinking* about the meaning of the dream. What I felt was not so much a new direction for my life but a confirmation that my plans were not misplaced. I was headed the right way with my life.

Shortly after our break at the retreat center, the practical field course ended. SIL was unable to obtain permissions or visas for Central Asia at that time, and our language survey was postponed. I returned from the Philippines with excellent evaluations from SIL on my language-learning skills and community involvement interests. They also suggested that these two pursuits conflicted with language analysis settings. In other words, it was obviously easy for me to learn new languages, but I also enjoyed being with people rather than sitting at a desk doing language analysis. So they encouraged me to pursue opportunities for service in a cross-cultural relief agency. I returned to the United States with a greater desire to serve God but still no means to get to Afghanistan—the place I felt called to serve.

So Close and Yet So Far

Back home in North Carolina, God gave me some beautiful relationships with the Russian refugee community near us in Asheville. In fact, such a unique bond developed with the Gundorin family that, in the summer of 1997, we journeyed together to Germany, Belarus, and Russia. Vladimir invited me to go with his family to visit churches in the former Soviet Union.

He introduced me to that part of the world at ground level. We traveled in a Volvo through Germany, Belarus, and Russia. I remember vividly a service at one Russian church. As I walked to the pulpit to make a few remarks, I was kissed on the lips several times by the leaders of the church. As a single American guy, I don't get kissed a lot, especially not on the lips by other guys. So it was an eye-opening cultural experience for me.

We spent many long days in that Volvo, because the Russian countryside is as wide as it is beautiful. Eventually we arrived in Vladikovkos, near the Caucasus Mountains in southern Russia. The house church that Vladimir had started several years before was doing well. We had come to the end of our journey.

My mind frequently drifted to Afghanistan during those days. I learned that Afghanistan was still a painful subject to Russians, much as Vietnam was in the U.S. during the seventies and eighties. Still, I asked the Russian Christians to pray for the people of Afghanistan, their recent enemy. At that point, only the Caspian Sea and Turkmenistan lay between my goal and me. Once again I was close, but I couldn't get there. We finally said our farewells and returned to the States.

SCOUTING OUT THE LAND

From January to May of 1998, I studied hard and received a master of arts degree in intercultural studies from Columbia International University. As the school year wound down, I learned of a team of friends who were going on a survey trip to Turkey, Turkmenistan, and Uzbekistan to explore opportunities for service. Their departure date coincided nicely with my graduation, and I liked the idea of "scouting out the land." So I decided to join them. To my excitement and delight, we even included in our plan the possibility of visiting the bordering country of Afghanistan.

We traveled from west to east across Central Asia—Turkey, Armenia, Azerbaijan, Turkmenistan, and Uzbekistan. I enjoyed the region as much as I had dreamed I would. We observed the cultures, noted the similarities and differences within the region, and absorbed all the exotic sights, sounds, and tastes of that part of the world. Along the way, we also did some teacher training of local instructors in ESL (English as a Second Language) or EFL (English as a Foreign Language). Most of us had been trained to do this. We also interviewed a number of teams that were already doing relief and development work in the area. We wanted to get a sense of what needs were already being met, which ones weren't, and how we might participate.

We eventually arrived in Termiz, Uzbekistan, by train. As a border crossing, the city lived under tight military restrictions. Residual animosity existed between Afghanistan and Uzbekistan since much of the previous Russian military invasion and supply line ran through Termiz. Though open warfare had ended a decade before, and the Soviet Union was no longer in official control, the tensions and suspicions remained. Foreigners were under careful scrutiny, and the area was labeled a "security risk." Uzbek officials had good cause for concern, because the vicious Taliban had already announced their intention to conquer the neighboring countries once they controlled Afghanistan.

We visited Termiz for a week to do English teacher training at a university there. As soon as possible, we made our way to the border at Al-Termizi (a famous folk Islamic shrine that contains the body of a "holy man"), on the south side of Termiz.

I still remember the feelings of wonder and anticipation I had the first time I looked across the river and actually saw Afghanistan. The land was low and dry, but in the distance a row of mountains stretched left and right as far as the horizon. Shades of brown and gray colored the shorter mountains cascading toward me. The land seemed so alive! It called to me, like a siren of the sea. I wasn't there yet, but I was so much closer than ever before. At that moment, my heart became forever bound to that country, her people, and the God who created them.

STAYING TO SERVE

After that weeklong seminar, we returned to Tashkent, the capital. Our trip was at an end. The team, including me, was scheduled to return shortly to the States. While we were debriefing our experience as a team, I floated out the idea that I was considering staying in Uzbekistan. The trip had been a great learning exercise, but I wanted more. I was eager to begin investing myself in people's lives—to start filling in some of those gaps I knew existed. Besides, I had finished graduate school and had no other specific reasons to return to the States.

We discussed the idea at length, and while our leader reluctantly agreed with my motives, he suggested three wise conditions:

1. I needed to have the approval of my home church (my support base).
2. I needed to be released by the group that was sponsoring our team (my accountability structure).
3. I needed to be "adopted" by a team already established in the country (a new accountability structure).

Though feeling free-spirited and adventuresome, I agreed. I knew I needed some kind of support structure that could help me with contacts, provide accountability, and give me a place for teamwork. Fortunately, all three conditions were met almost immediately. Back home, my family and friends enthusiastically gave me their support. My summer team released me. And a new team adopted me—it was affiliated with Development, Aid, Relief and Education (DARE), based out of the United Kingdom.

DARE is influential in placing hundreds of Christian professionals in Central Asia. Their focus is to provide relief, education, and development services where needed. They link teachers and other qualified professionals with specific openings in various countries. They often loan (or second) their staff to other agencies for special duties and opportunities. I knew the organization. They had assisted the Kurds during the Gulf War and the people of Turkey after devastating earthquakes. For the young renegade in me, DARE provides accountability, support, and guidance.

I joined a group of teachers who had been preparing to teach English at the University of Termiz. We had an invitation to teach, with the promise of a twenty-dollar monthly salary, but we had no housing. In fact, foreigners were not permitted to actually live in Termiz, because of its strategic location on the border. So we asked friends to join us in praying for a solution. To our surprise, we soon received special permission from the president of Uzbekistan to live in Termiz and teach English at the university. We had no political clout. The president was simply acting on behalf of his country's desperate need to catch up with the rest of the world. He wanted English to be taught. I arrived back at the border of Afghanistan long before I imagined, and I had a wonderful year of teaching, learning, and tasting Central Asia.

Then, ten months later, in the spring of 1999, local restrictions tightened again, and we were asked to leave. We had several opportunities during that school year to share our faith. But I became keenly aware of how sensitive an issue the gospel is in a nation that officially claims a different religion. I paid frequent visits to the border, lifting my hands to pray for peace in Afghanistan, asking God to open a door for me to go where my heart already seemed to be living. I repeatedly asked God for the privilege to serve Him among the Afghan people. But the door remained firmly closed.

I left Termiz and then Uzbekistan feeling disappointed and frustrated. I was so close I could at times actually smell Afghanistan. I couldn't help but wonder when and how I would ever get inside the country I wanted so badly to serve.

A Dream Comes True

BACK IN THE STATES, I spent the last half of 1999 serving in the beautiful mountains of western North Carolina at Mount Bethel Church, a fellowship that has supported me for years. The followers of Christ in this area have provided shelter, guidance, and a connecting point for my faith each time I returned to the States. While ministering there in familiar territory I waited for Afghanistan to call and, like the Macedonians, say, "Come over and help us."

THAILAND—In February 2000, I was invited to the Central Asian Conference in Thailand, which included many of the people, ministries, and agencies serving in that region. As I planned for this event, I also discovered a school in Thailand that offers a certificate course called Teaching English to Speakers of Other Languages (TESOL). *How convenient and ironic,* I thought: *My best opportunity to serve the people of Afghanistan may depend on my willingness simply to teach my own native language.* The Thailand trip now had two important purposes: to sharpen my skills as a teacher and to meet with others who were exploring options for service in Central Asia.

The first stop on my itinerary was Ban Phe, Thailand, a beautiful island area south of Bangkok. I attended Trinity University, Thailand, an extension of a larger institution based in London, England. The school offers courses for people to earn English-teaching certificates around the world. I enjoyed the setting as well as the course, and my teaching skills received some helpful polishing. The experience also reminded me of how much I enjoy teaching.

THE DOOR BEGINS TO OPEN

Next, I flew up to Chiang Mai, Thailand, for the Central Asia Conference. I tried not to think too hopefully about the doors that might open for me during the conference. After all, my previous efforts to get into Afghanistan had failed, and this might be just another dead end. At the same time, I wanted to, in the words of my Muslim friends, "Trust God's wisdom and timing."

One morning during the conference, I had breakfast with Norm Leatherwood, executive director of Shelter Now International, based in the United States, and Randall Olson, then regional director for SNI/Central Asia. They introduced me to the vision and work of their agency, SNI/Shelter for Life. They also filled me in on the details of their activities in northern Afghanistan.

During 1998 and 1999, programs focused primarily on dealing with the emergency relief and immediate shelter needs of people left homeless by the civil war and severe earthquakes. Norm and Rand also described other long-term needs that were crying for attention. For instance, SNI/SFL hoped to expand into areas of education and community development.

While talking to Norm and Rand, I remembered that I had heard about SNI's response to the 1998 earthquakes in northern Afghanistan. I recalled meetings in Uzbekistan to pray for the victims and those launching the relief efforts. A friend of mine had even said, "John, this may be your chance." I considered approaching SNI about being involved then, but I didn't pursue it, because I still had a commitment in Termiz that I thought might lead to contacts in Afghanistan.

As it turned out, Norm and Rand knew about my situation in Termiz and had even made some preliminary contacts to recruit some of our team for their emergency relief response in Afghanistan. They reminded me of a general e-mail they sent from Tajikistan to ask if anyone would be willing to "come over and help us." Though it had been a good idea, the timing had been wrong for me then. However, a lot had changed since then.

Talking to them was almost like being there. How sweet it was to listen to the stories of those who had actually lived and worked inside Afghanistan. Rand finally asked me if I still wanted to serve in Afghanistan. I told him I was ready to leave the next day.

He responded, "Well, we need someone immediately in Feyzabad to teach English at the medical school. You actually could go tomorrow. We already have an office there, but you would be responsible to start the program."

I could hardly believe my ears! The door to Afghanistan was finally opening. I didn't know whether to shout or cry. I quickly told them I was definitely interested but would need to talk with my family and get clearance from DARE and the green light from my support team. I assured them they would hear back from me shortly.

BLESSINGS FROM HOME

NORTH CAROLINA—I was so excited I hardly needed an airplane to fly back to the States. My home church gave their enthusiastic blessing. Other friends, mentors, and counselors chuckled and said such things as, "Well, it's about time." My family, though concerned, was not too surprised, and they eagerly gave their support. DARE, which was providing my financial structure and accountability, also agreed that this was a good match for me and gladly assigned me for service with SNI/Shelter for Life. I checked with people who had experience with SNI/SFL and got the thumbs up from them.

I contacted the SNI/SFL international office in Oshkosh, Wisconsin, to complete the application process. Within days, I was accepted. As promised, they scheduled me to fly to Dushanbe, Tajikistan, since it was the home of their regional office for all of Central Asia. I expected to receive some field training and orientation when I reached Tajikistan.

I ticked off my short to-do list. One application for a visa for Tajikistan (permission to enter the country) filled out and mailed. Flights arranged; tickets purchased. Contact friends for visits along the way. All the tasks ran smoothly. I packed and repacked. I was as antsy to get started as a racehorse at the starting gate. But weeks passed, and no Tajik visa appeared. Veterans at Shelter for Life assured me that snags often happen and not to get discouraged. So I followed their normal procedure—go ahead and start the trip, and check on the visa along the way.

REJECTED!

BERLIN—I made stops in London, Amsterdam, and Berlin. At each place I phoned home to check on my Tajik visa. I had reapplied twice while I was waiting, thinking my paperwork might have gotten lost. By the time I reached Berlin, the visa rejection slips had begun arriving at home—three of them. They came without explanations. I have never known the reason behind those rejections.

Fortunately, Tajikistan has a local embassy in Berlin. The friends I stayed with gave me directions and sent me off alone on the subway to submit my fourth application for a Tajik visa. A trip on a subway is normally an enjoyable adventure for me, but I dreaded that one. I tried not to think of those three rejection notices in baseball terms— I hoped I hadn't struck out. I approached the embassy half expecting to find wanted posters with my face on them hanging in the building. I couldn't imagine why they would deny me permission to enter the country when all I wanted to do was help.

Even though Tajikistan is no longer under the rule of Communism, it remains a difficult country to access. I entered the embassy, introduced myself, and asked for a visa application. The woman at the counter was courteous and friendly. She readily gave me the forms, which I filled out there in the office. She didn't even raise an eyebrow when I handed in the application and told her I was willing to pay for express service, because I was scheduled on the next flight out of Munich in a few days. She nodded. She knew about that flight. When only one weekly international flight enters your country, you might conclude that few people want to visit. She told me to return in an hour.

I spent that eternal hour nervously scribbling thank-you notes to people who had been so supportive in recent weeks. In addition to being a way to stay connected with family and friends, writing has always been therapeutic for me. I returned to the embassy an hour later, and to my surprise and thrill, the visa was approved and ready. No questions, no hassles. They gave me an invoice for one hundred fifty dollars. As the official handed me the approved visa, my mind's eye watched another barrier between Afghanistan and me collapse.

On the Road Again

MUNICH TO DUSHANBE—Two days later I took the same subway to the airport for my flight south to Munich. I relaxed. The hiss of the doors and the rumble of the wheels announced the beginning of my Afghanistan adventure. I was finally on my way to a land without subways or the electricity to run them. My flight from Berlin to Munich covered three hundred miles of beautiful German landscape. And my flight from Munich to Dushanbe would carry me almost two thousand miles and two thousand years into a land anchored in the past. I knew the next few weeks would be filled with culture shock, change, and personal adjustment. I couldn't wait!

Boarding the Russian-made Tupalov jet in Munich for the flight from Europe to Central Asia, I noticed that the contrasts between my flightmates were multimedia. The closer I came to my ultimate destination, the less people looked, sounded, and acted as I do. From every direction, I could hear snatches of exotic languages. Official announcements by the pilot and crew made it clear that I was now in that part of the world still bearing the indelible stamp of the Soviet Union. Russian remains the trade language. The pilot also made announcements in Tajik and a very unusual version of English. As I said a few words in Russian to my seatmate to be polite and respectful, a cloud of Turkish tobacco smoke filled the cabin. We buckled in for the trip, and I thought with a grin, *Well, Toto, we're not in Kansas anymore.*

Throughout the flight, I noticed people going by my seat in groups. Hissing noises occasionally reached my ears. Curious, I walked to the rear of the plane. In an open space behind the seats, I found people gathered around a roaring, butane stove, brewing tea. This was apparently a serve-yourself arrangement, and they welcomed me into their circle. I was about to ask if the captain was aware of the open flame in the back of his aircraft when the pilot himself joined us for a cup of tea. My feeling of safety began to wane.

The first leg of our journey took us from Munich, Germany, to Istanbul, Turkey. There I exchanged one set of interesting traveling companions for another. Ten hours after departure from Munich, we landed safely in Dushanbe. I noted the date in my journal: August 5, 2000.

MY HOME AWAY FROM HOME

DUSHANBE, TAJIKISTAN—A city with five million inhabitants, Dushanbe is the capital of Tajikistan. Isolated, surrounded, and even invaded by mountains, Dushanbe illustrates the uniqueness of the country. It may contain more mountains per square mile than any place on earth. And the resulting valleys provide meager opportunities for farming.

Under the Soviet system, most of Tajikistan's arable land was assigned to cotton production. Those responsible for raising cotton paid little attention to soil conservation. Consequently, Tajikistan ranks among the poorest nations on earth. It shares many of the challenges of its southern neighbor. Our regional office oversees relief and development projects in northern Afghanistan from this base of operations in addition to addressing the enormous humanitarian needs inside Tajikistan itself.

I located a little apartment that was almost identical to my place in Termiz. The Soviets had built thousands of utilitarian concrete buildings, most of them seemingly built from the same blueprints. Ugly blocks of man-made stone enclose many rows and multi-leveled identical cubicles. Somehow they are made livable by the determined residents, who insist on adding touches of color, warmth, and personality to stone gray structures that appear designed to deny individuality and creativity. Personally, I was content with the shelter.

I soon met many refugees from Afghanistan. One I remember in particular. because his English was excellent. So I pumped him for enlightening information about his country. His story of how he fled from the Taliban was not only heartbreaking but also a good reminder of what millions of Afghans have suffered.

He was a medical student in Kabul when the civil war in Afghanistan broke out. Between the dangers of the war and the Taliban's hatred for education, my friend had fled for his life. Not long after that, his life took another turn: One of his sisters was being forced to marry a powerful man against her wishes. So he helped his mother, brother, and sisters escape, but then he lost contact with them. When I met him, he hadn't seen his family for years, though he had recently discovered their whereabouts and had talked with them by phone. I was happy for him. And there was another thing about him that forged an instant bond between us: My first Afghan friend was a passionate follower of Jesus, the Messiah.

A CRASH COURSE

DUSHANBE—I met the rest of the SNI staff in Dushanbe and began a crash course on the structure, history, and scope of the organization's involvement in Central Asia. I counted down the days, impatiently awaiting my first excursion into northern Afghanistan, but I had to wait a few weeks before boarding the UN plane headed south. I knew I needed the field orientation. Besides, I had to get over my first bout with the stomach bug we affectionately call the "central Asian weight loss program." I also needed an Afghan visa. SNI was trying to extend my Tajik visa to a one-year, multiple-entry permit, so that I could travel in and out of Afghanistan. I had good reasons to stay put.

Meanwhile, I met with two language helpers. One, a Tajik woman, helped me learn some basic Tajik and Uzbek. Tajikistan is full of Uzbeks, thanks to Stalin and the Russians, who divided up Central Asia without considering ethnic territories. My other language instructor, a man from Kabul, helped me learn some simple Dari phrases. He insisted that I learn the alphabet, which was frustrating to me.

I kept saying, "Babies don't learn the alphabet first. They learn to say 'goo goo' and 'gaa gaa' before anything else."

Unfortunately, my classes were less than ideal and only lasted a couple of weeks. They abruptly ended when the regional director of SNI announced our first trip south. There were problems with one of the projects we had in place, and the director needed to intervene. He asked me to come along for a quick look at the country. At last! I was going to Afghanistan.

As I prepared for my arrival in Afghanistan, I mentally reviewed the difficult history of these people. Afghanistan has tasted some unspeakable trials during the past decade.

A Colorful and Tragic History

AFGHANISTAN—A cruel civil war that broke out in 1996 ravaged the country. And years of drought conditions showed no signs of ending. Herds of cattle died, and farmers were driven away by their parched lands. Cities swelled as desperate refugees with their children fled the ruthless fighting and starvation. Millions of Afghans escaped across the borders into Pakistan and Iran.

Then, devastating earthquakes hit northern Afghanistan in 1998, causing thousands of roofs to collapse onto innocent, sleeping victims. More than seven thousand Afghans lost their lives, and over fifty thousand homes were destroyed or left unlivable.

The people of Afghanistan have, in my opinion, experienced more than their share of suffering and violent death. Land mines continually maim and kill innocent victims with their deadly, unannounced explosions. Reports indicate there are still multitudes of them scattered around the countryside. Thousands of Afghans are now lame or handicapped because of them. It seems that wherever two or three are gathered in Afghanistan, at least one of them uses crutches.

In areas where famine relentlessly stalks its sunken-faced victims, and drought chokes the life out of dehydrating people, destitute widows and orphans survive only by begging in the streets. Millions of the homeless and hungry have spent frigid winters in barely inhabitable refugee camps. In truth, most animals in America live in better conditions than these stricken people.

Statistics show that one in four children in Afghanistan dies before the age of five. Those who somehow manage to grow up receive little or no education, because school buildings have become convenient headquarters and barracks for soldiers and military personnel.

Meanwhile, the average life expectancy of Afghan adults is about forty-six years, compared to seventy-six in America. The whole human psyche and dignity of thousands of Afghans has been damaged or nearly destroyed. Over two million people have been killed in the war or died of malnutrition, disease, or exposure to the elements since the Russian Invasion of 1979.

AT THE CROSSROADS

Afghanistan's string of problems, though, goes even further back than 1979. When speaking of the length of conflicts, wars, and invasions, Afghanistan's troubles are measured in centuries, not in decades. Since it is situated between the Middle East and Asia, Afghanistan is the natural crossroads of ancient trade and invasion routes.

Alexander the Great traveled Afghanistan's rugged mountains in the fourth century B.C. The Book of Ezra in the Bible speaks of Cyrus and the Persian Empire of the sixth century B.C. After the time of Christ, Arab and Mongol conquerors fought over this area. Marco Polo passed through Afghanistan in the late 1200s on his way to China and recorded the disastrous ruin and bleak beauty of the land. He even visited Feyzabad, where I live.

In 1747, the modern State of Afghanistan was created when Ahmad Shah Durrani united rival Afghan tribes. The first of three Anglo-Afghan wars occurred from 1838 through 1842. This British invasion was designed to counteract Russian expansion.

Other wars followed. The struggle for power and geography between Russia and Britain became known as the Great Game. It continued until 1878. Afghanistan and Britain finally signed a treaty in 1879, but England retained control of international policy.

Modern history also shows that many others have expressed curious interest in this country that borders six others. In fact, on the map it appears to be the very heart of Central Asia.

SNAPSHOTS OF AFGHANISTAN

Other characteristics help to draw a clearer picture of this nation known as the Land of the Afghans. Similar in size to the state of Texas and home to more than twenty million people, Afghanistan features remarkable ethnic diversity. The population is made up of four sizable people groups—Pashtun, Tajik, Hazara, and Uzbek—and some eight other significant minority groups. The Durand Line, or eastern border dividing Afghanistan and British India, was established in 1895. That border splits the Pashtun ethnic group, leaving half of them in what is now Pakistan. The northern border divides lands traditionally held by Uzbeks and Tajiks. Sadly, the nation's ethnic diversity has historically sparked more violence than strength.

Afghanistan finally became an independent state in 1919, after Britain signed a treaty giving up all interest. However, just ten years later, in 1929, a civil war broke out when conservative Islamic forces reacted against Amir Amanullah Khan's modern social reforms.

Then, for about forty years, Afghanistan experienced at least a taste of peace under the reign of King Mohammad Zahir Shah (1933–1973). However, border disputes with Pakistan aroused bitter strife in the 1960s, which ultimately led to Mohammed Daoud's seizing power in a coup in 1973. But he was assassinated in 1978 under Mohammad Taraki's pro-Soviet coup. Then, in 1979, Taraki was assassinated by Amin, who soon lost his life in yet another Communist-led coup.

MEET THE MUJAHIDIN

The invasion by Russia birthed the rebel movement that became known as the Mujahidin. These guerrilla forces launched a war and soon received arms and support from the U.S., Pakistan, China, Egypt, Iran, and Saudi Arabia for their struggle against the Soviet Union. Uncounted thousands of Afghan civilians died in that struggle. During this war, which raged until 1985, millions of Afghans were driven from their homes and their beloved country.

Najibullah came to power in 1986. By then, the U.S. had armed the Mujahidin with Stinger missiles, so they could shoot down Soviet helicopter gunships. General Massoud became famous during those days as he led the resistance movement in the Panjshir and other areas of Afghanistan. It's even possible that Osama bin Laden entered the country at this time.

Finally, in 1988, the United States, Afghanistan, Pakistan, and the USSR signed a peace treaty that led to the withdrawal of Soviet troops. The last Soviet forces left Afghanistan sometime in 1989, the same year that the U.S. Embassy closed in Kabul.

Unfortunately, external peace treaties did little to heal the deep divisions within the country. The Pashtuns actually have a pessimistic saying that describes their own character: "We are at peace when we are at war." The Mujahidin, many of them Pashtuns, continued fighting Najibullah, the Soviet puppet. They took Kabul in 1992. This allowed Burhanuddin Rabbani, an ethnic Tajik, to rise to the position of president. But various factions within the country continued to fight.

Kabul reeled under an awful blow in 1994 when civil broke out over control of the city. It resulted from a power struggle between Prime Minister Gulbuddin Hekmatyar and President Rabbani. Rocket, mortar, and artillery fire from the surrounding hills left many areas of the capital city in ruins. So many homes and businesses had their roofs destroyed that the overhead view of parts of the city looked like miniature mud canyons, devoid of life. Regretably, thousands more died.

OSAMA BIN LADEN AND TALIBAN TERROR

The Taliban emerged during this time. Most of them were young, fanatical Muslims trained in a version of Islam that condones almost unlimited violence to establish control. The Taliban proved to be fearless, ruthless fighters. They set up operations after capturing Kandahar, the largest southeastern city near the border of Pakistan. The Taliban leader was Mullah Omar, their official interpreter of what they purport to be the *correct* teachings of Islam.

In 1996, the Taliban seized control of Kabul by driving out Rabbani and killing Najibullah. At this time they began to enforce their strict Islamic code on the entire population. Women were deprived of most of their rights and required to wear the traditional head-to-toe covering when in public. Girls lost the opportunity for education, and most schools were closed, because the Taliban believe that nothing but the Koran needs to be studied. Punishment for even minor infractions was severe. Public beatings, hangings, and gun executions became common.

Osama bin Laden was definitely now in Afghanistan. His plans for worldwide terrorism and the Taliban's view of life formed a deadly alliance. The Taliban, aided by outsiders, threatened to overrun the country. Rabbani, the internationally recognized president, was now limited to his capital in Feyzabad. The two most northern provinces of the country, Takhar and Badakhshan, gradually became the only stronghold of the Northern Alliance. Their military leadership rested in the hands and abilities of Ahmad Shah Massoud. So the war dragged on.

In 1998, northern Afghanistan made worldwide news when it was rocked by a series of devastating earthquakes. Until that time, the world had basically ignored the political turmoil in the country, but the natural disaster begged for humanitarian response. This devastating earthquake rousted many outside the country to awareness of the critical needs in the region.

EMERGENCY ASSISTANCE

Some help was close by. SNI/Shelter for Life International had been working in neighboring Tajikistan since 1994. The post-Soviet government had welcomed relief groups that were willing to respect the Islamic traditions in the country while providing much needed help at little cost. Several staff members were living and serving in the country. Building projects were up and running, providing emergency housing. Shelter for Life was one of the first agencies contacted to help respond to the emergency in mountainous areas of northeast Afghanistan.

Harry Van Burik and Joe Settle of SNI flew from Tajikistan into northern Afghanistan to assess the situation on behalf of a number of relief agencies anxious to help. Sometime during the trip, it occurred to them that they were flying into a war zone in a Russian helicopter. They were never fired upon, but they faced a host of AK-47s as soldiers of the Northern Alliance greeted them. But since they had come to help, they were welcomed with gladness and gratitude. They were among the first outsiders to witness and survey the extensive earthquake damage and were also instrumental in setting into motion an effective international relief effort.

As large an area as Central Asia is, the population of outsiders tends to be an obvious minority. Groups involved in relief and development work, for example, all know each other. They regularly coordinate their efforts. Because resources tend to be limited, groups have to decide whether they are going to compete or cooperate. In order to meet the desperate needs in the area, cooperation is the only workable policy. Often, there's really no other choice.

SNI/Shelter for Life has worked hard to gain the respect of other agencies by its practices, programs, and willingness to serve others. We have often been able to place trained staff in areas where other agencies have only been able to transport significant amounts of relief materials. Agencies like USAID and the UN relief units often have massive quantities of emergency supplies and huge international delivery systems, but they rely on locally based distribution agencies that are familiar with a region. This assures that the relief materials actually get to the people who really need it. In 1998, SNI/Shelter for Life was the only international Christian-based relief and development organization serving in northeastern Afghanistan.

For many reasons, U.S.-based SNI began to use the name Shelter for Life to identify its work in Afghanistan. Years of experience in emergency relief work caused the leadership in SNI to reconsider the importance of community development in responding to crises. The name "Shelter Now" was chosen originally to emphasize the urgency of the needs the organization was created to address. It was a descriptive name. When a crisis occurs somewhere in the world, those affected need help *now*. They need food *now*. They need medical assistance, blankets, and clothing *now*. They need shelter *now*.

As SNI actually became involved in responding to affected areas in the world, the organization learned that, once critical needs have been met after a disaster or war, a whole new set of needs arises for the displaced:

- Should they return home?
- Should they settle permanently in a new location?
- If their homes have been damaged or destroyed by the elements or the fighting, what can be done to provide permanent housing for them?
- What should be done about disrupted schools, local government, bombed buildings, ongoing drought, destroyed or nonexistent water supplies, waste management, roads, and medical facilities?

Bottom line: Those who have survived need sustained help to re-establish the cherished place they call home. Refugees need ongoing assistance in rebuilding their lives, hopes, and dreams. They need help in creating a means to provide food for themselves and their families. They need established clinics, jobs, security, and help with various facets of community development.

The fact is, they need *shelter for life*. The new name, Shelter for

Life, seems to more accurately describe the total vision of the founders, who began Shelter Now International back in the 1980s. The original team dreamed of an effective Christian relief organization that could offer both immediate assistance and help for the long road of recovery and development in the most needy places.

Afghanistan is exactly the kind of place Shelter for Life was born to serve. The more I understood the history of the need in this country and the response SNI/Shelter for Life had already given, the more I was excited to participate with them. So, with visas stamped in my passport, a UN plane ticket in my pocket, and a passion in my heart, I eagerly anticipated finally standing inside Afghanistan.

A Bend in the Road

FEYZABAD, AFGHANISTAN—The trip by air from Dushanbe to Feyzabad takes a little over an hour. An eight-passenger aircraft operated by the United Nations offers a no-frills, all-thrills ride through one of the most scenic areas of the world. After all my hours of jet travel, the propeller blades and piston engines provided an exhilarating sense of flight. Our revved-up butterfly climbed steeply out of the Tajik capital. Invisible hands seemed to toy with our tiny craft as we passed through the turbulent mountain air.

Even at twenty thousand feet, our little plane was dwarfed by mountain peaks rising majestically above us. Fortunately, we flew between the peaks that we couldn't fly over. As our plane descended through the rough terrain of Badakhshan province in Afghanistan, I looked through the airplane windows, speechless.

The countryside was obviously bone dry, even from the air, but the scenery was still breathtaking. Afghanistan in September displayed multiple hues of browns and grays with hints of green in the valleys. Although the last of the gleaming summit snows shone above, melting to quench the parched lands below, the fields remained thirsty. And the massive, rocky waves of the Hindu Kush Range lined up in front of us all the way to the horizon.

As we flew south, I looked out the east windows to my left and imagined that I could see the borderlands of China's western frontier. Out the west side of the plane, I saw the rolling hills and flatlands towards Mazar-e Sharif, where I knew people were dying—some from war and some from hunger and exposure.

Northeast Afghanistan shares many topographical similarities with Colorado. The transition between lofty peaks and deep valleys, mountain meadows and desert scrublands happens quickly. A single picture rarely captures the extremes.

As we flew over the well-worn pathways of history, I imagined all the armies that had fought and died in the valleys and passes below us—Carthaginians, Arabs, Mongols, Britains, Russians, and generation after generation of Afghans. I wondered how people who have always known violence manage to carry on with their day-to-day lives.

TOUCHDOWN

Our wheels touched the ground, and I was immediately stunned by powerful visual reminders of the most recent wars. Destroyed buildings, blown-up Russian tanks and vehicles, and charred aircraft surrounded the airport runway. We had landed in a military junkyard.

Climbing down the metal stairs from the tiny airplane, I stepped onto Afghan soil at long last. I breathed in the dust and pungent aromas that would quickly become familiar to me. The late morning chill announced cold days ahead, and I shivered, because I had come unprepared for the cold. All I carried was a small bag of necessities and the clothes I had on, but I couldn't stop grinning. *This is just a short visit anyway; I'll pack more clothes next time,* I thought. I had finally arrived. I was *in* Afghanistan!

"Thank you, Lord," I prayed with every breath. "Allow me to bring some of your peace and blessing to this land."

A crowd of little shepherd boys ran toward the plane, laughing—so much for airport security. They were as curious about us newcomers as I was of them. Their flocks, accustomed to airplane noises and perhaps more violent ones, grazed unsupervised as the boys examined us. I returned the compliment. Their bright, dark eyes, dazzling smiles, and colorful clothing captured my attention. I took a mental snapshot, because I wanted to memorize that wonderful moment.

I couldn't help but notice two little boys who lagged behind the others, because each one ran on only one foot aided by a crude crutch. Their empty pant legs dangled pitifully in the breeze. The ravages of war were obviously recorded on more than rusted-out airplane hulks and pockmarked buildings. They were also carved into the mine-blasted bodies of Afghan children.

Not really knowing what else to do, I greeted them in the first language that came to mind—Uzbek. To my delight, they understood me and gleefully responded. Their unexpected chorus caught me by surprise. I knew that many ethnic Uzbeks live in the north of Afghanistan, but this was a wonderful way to confirm that fact. I was able to share a simple conversation my first day in the country. Suddenly those months in Termiz, Uzbekistan, took on a whole new significance. I had taken a year of language training for this very moment.

DUAL-PURPOSE PLAN

Our regional director had made it very clear that we had two purposes for this quick trip. First, we needed to meet with local officials to clarify our role in northern Afghanistan as an international Christian relief and development agency. That discussion would primarily be held in Rostaq, where our central office was located. Our original relief work in the region involved shelter reconstruction after the 1998 earthquakes.

Recently we had been asked to do increasingly more relief work with displaced people in other areas. Thousands of people were homeless and wandering the streets and roads because of the war and tyranny initiated by the Taliban. Sadly, this crisis showed no signs of ending. Needs cried out for attention everywhere. But we had to clarify our role and make sure we had permission to continue our work as a Christian agency working in a Muslim country.

It is common for followers of Christ who serve in similar settings to be questioned about their motives. I compare it to the tension faced at times by Jews, Muslims, and Christians teaching in the public school systems in the Unites States. They teach under certain restrictions. As I understand it, the issue isn't that they can't share their faith; the issue is that they can't require their students to listen. They can't use their class as a captive audience to teach their religious views, any more than an atheist would be allowed to enforce unbelief on students. We carry out our roles as relief workers under the same restrictions. To expand our involvement in Afghanistan, we needed to clarify the expectations of local author-ities and assure them of our cooperation.

The second objective of our trip into northern Afghanistan depended on the first. If we found continued favor with authori-ties, the director and I planned to stay in the country for several more days. We wanted to conduct a quick survey of the area, noting places and needs that might require both short-term and long-term projects by Shelter for Life.

My specific task was to evaluate the challenges of expanding our work into areas of education. I was slated to teach English at a local college in Feyzabad. However, under these wartime and extreme drought conditions, we knew other things demanded our attention. In fact, we were not yet in a position to launch educa-tional projects, though I was eager to begin. On this trip, we were seeking enough information to create my plan of action for serving in Afghanistan.

I thought about these objectives as we walked from the airplane to our ride. I couldn't help but remark about a spray-painted decla-ration in English on the mud wall of a bombed-out building not far from the runway. I read the sign aloud, "Opium Is against Islam."

The director chuckled and said, "You should have been here a few months ago. Right under that sign and all around that building I saw a bumper crop of opium growing. I guess the farmer couldn't read English."

The director waved to our driver, who leaped from a Russian Jeep and welcomed us to the country. Our bags went quickly into the back of the Jeep, and we sped away. I wondered what the hurry was until the director leaned forward and said above the roar, "If we get away first, we won't have to eat everyone else's dust on the way into town." I looked back and could no longer see the airplane or any of the other vehicles. They were lost in a billowing red cloud that seemed to be chasing us down the road.

When we arrived at our little four-room office in Feyzabad, we were graciously greeted by some of our local staff. They had hot tea waiting for us, which we welcomed with gratitude. We could also smell the traditional lamb kabob and rice pilaf cooking.

Bolstered by my linguistic success at the airport, I tried imme-diately to communicate with our staff. Unlike my little shepherd friends, however, none of them spoke Uzbek. They were all ethnic Tajiks. So, undaunted, I switched to my few phrases of Dari (the Afghan version of Farsi) that I had picked up in Dushanbe. They understood! I could see the excitement in their eyes. *Here's a foreigner who speaks Dari,* they probably thought. They began to respond rapidly to my simple greetings only to discover that I spoke just a few words of Dari. But we had a beginning.

A Bazaar Experience

That first day in Feyzabad, we went shopping. The market in any city or town in Central Asia serves as the mall where everyone goes to get life's essentials and catch up on the news. They call the places "bazaars," a term we have borrowed to enrich English. These are wonderful, smelly, noisy places where you can sense the liveliness of a culture. These were the world's first supermarkets—full of animals, traders, moneychangers, and Afghans of varied ethnic stock buying, selling, and making a living.

Before I could shop, though, I had to visit a moneychanger's booth. Banks are rare in Afghanistan, but moneychangers abound. Almost anyone with a little extra liquidity gets involved in the exchange business. When I arrived in the country, the going rate allowed me to exchange a U.S. dollar for fifteen of the most common currency bill, the Afghani ten-thousand note. That means a one-hundred-fifty-thousand-to-one exchange rate. Even small purchases in the bazaar require rubber-banded bricks of currency.

I bought an Afghan outfit called *showakamis* at one of the clothing stalls. Though it was different from the clothes my Kurdish friends taught me to wear, I immediately felt comfortable in it. Traditional Afghan clothing for a man consists of very loose pants made from light cloth—similar to what we call pajama bottoms in the States. The waist of the pants is more than twice the size of the wearer's midsection, but the fabric is gathered and held up by a drawstring. Over these pants, men wear a loose-fitting pullover shirt with very long tails front and back. These look a little like linen nightshirts, but the sides are sown in an eye-pleasing arch, rather than slit from bottom to waist.

Depending on the temperature, men also wear a light wrap or blanket over their shoulders that can be used to shield the face and head or provide an extra layer around the shoulders on a chilly morning. This colorful scarf also serves as a prayer rug when an Afghan stops somewhere other than a mosque for one of Islam's daily five prayer times.

In northern Afghanistan, men often also wear a hat called a *pakul,* made popular by General Massoud. The heavy wool cap has a flat top and rolled-up sides. Many men wear other traditional forms of the rolled-up headdress or round hats that bear the color and shape of their tribal heritage. Most of my Uzbek friends wear a hat shaped like an upside-down bowl with a slightly pointed top. Sometimes they wrap a turban around it, creating the most recognizable head covering in the Middle East. The colors of their hats are a mixture of red, green, black, and various shades of gold and silver.

These clothing and headgear styles have been worn in this part of the world for many centuries. Contrary to most Westerners' opinions, they are functional and comfortable. My Muslim friends and I work, sleep, and live in these outfits.

MEDICALLY SPEAKING

Our Feyzabad stay lasted only a day and a half. We visited the medical college where I expected to teach English. The fact that this school welcomes both men and women for higher education made it the only one of its kind in Afghanistan at the time. I was looking forward to the privilege of helping these local Afghans, who were serving their country.

Next door we walked through the only hospital in the entire region where I saw my first military and civilian casualties of the war. Plainly, the facility was barely able to keep up with the demand for medical attention. Every bed was full. The doctors and nurses were far outnumbered by their patients. The ever-present wailing of the grief-stricken reminded us that death was no stranger here. A softer, almost mournful sound also reached my ears—Muslim prayers. This depressing place of dying promoted an urgent atmosphere for prayer. We prayed too.

Our medical escort told us that many of the villages in northern Afghanistan have basic medical clinics, but they struggle daily with critical shortages of even the most common medicines and trained health-care workers. With most of the medical resources dedicated to the war, the Northern Alliance found it nearly impossible to maintain their nation's health-care system.

We also visited some of the other relief offices like World Food Programme (WFP), United Nations Office for Coordination of Humanitarian Affairs (UNOCHA), International Committee of the Red Cross (ICRC), United Nations Children's Fund (UNICEF), Swedish Committee of Afghanistan (SCA), and others. These were all agencies with whom we worked in close cooperation. I had no idea how familiar I would become with all these offices in the coming months.

THE ROAD TO ROSTAQ

FEYZABAD TO ROSTAQ—Leaving Feyzabad, we drove west to Rostaq in our less-than-trusty Russian Jeep, a lasting and useful legacy of the Soviet occupation. I quickly discovered these are rugged and surly vehicles; their suspensions make up in durability what they lack in comfort. Another feature of these Jeeps is that the windows don't roll down, which is why they're called "traveling saunas" or, conversely, "freezers on wheels," depending on the season.

The roads we traveled reminded me of driving across the furrows of a cornfield in North Carolina—dry, bumpy, and dusty. The term "road" is almost always an overstatement in Afghanistan. These are narrow mountain trails used for centuries by camels and horses. They have been slightly widened for wheeled traffic. The results are sometimes dangerous. Vehicles often fail the test.

That first trip from Feyzabad to Rostaq was my nerve-racking introduction to Afghanistan travel. We even broke down once. But our talented and experienced Afghan driver was also a good mechanic, so he soon had us running and back on the road. Otherwise, we would have been stuck for who knows how long. (I've never seen a tow truck in northern Afghanistan. And with no phones, whom can you call?)

A Field Report

ROSTAQ—Our central field office is located in the mountainous village of Rostaq. This area, consisting of more than one hundred fifty villages, was the epicenter of the disastrous 1998 earthquake. We met our local staff, who are mostly Tajik. Some of them have been with our office since 1998, and three of them speak fairly fluent English.

Once again we were treated as royally as kings and welcomed with the finest hospitality. Soon they were telling us stories of their work since the earthquake, mostly for my benefit. I watched the expressions on their faces as they described the daunting tasks of rescue, relief, and reconstruction in which they had participated since the catastrophe. They practically glowed! I could tell they were fiercely proud of their efforts.

In the previous two years, hundreds of homes had been repaired or rebuilt. Damaged houses now had roofs, children had schools, and families had safe drinking water. People whose lives had been shattered now had shelter and hope.

These men exuded the kind of confidence and camaraderie that develops among people who have to depend on each other during crises. They struck me as ideal companions for a hazardous journey. I have since discovered that my first impression about them was accurate.

We also discussed the upcoming talks with the local authorities about our future plans. Here the staff expressed concern. The war loomed as a major obstacle to the future. The front line of the war was creeping ever closer. Communities that had just dug themselves out of the rubble of a natural disaster suddenly faced a new threat from the storms of war.

We also knew that part of the complicated conversations we were about to have with political and religious leaders grew out of tensions created when a Christian organization works in a strictly

Muslim area. Fortunately, we had a good track record of humanitarian service to hold up against some vague accusations and suspicions that had been falsely leveled against us.

I didn't envy the local leaders, because they had a difficult choice to make. They could ask us to leave, based on unsubstantiated charges of anti-Islamic activities, and thereby gain prestige as preservers of their faith. And, in fact, we had given them our word that we would go if they asked us to leave. However, they also realized that our departure would end every relief and development project we currently managed there. The fact of the matter was that there weren't any candidates for our replacement; no other humanitarian organization could step up as our substitute.

From our perspective, these discussions had to do with our integrity. For them, this was an opportunity to exercise wise and courageous leadership. They would either bow to prejudice or side with the pressing needs of their people. We hoped the lives and attitudes of our staff conveyed our deepest desire to serve.

A CRITICAL MEETING

Rostaq is actually full of ethnic Uzbeks. In fact, the local commander, the head religious elder, and the local governor were all Uzbek. At our first meeting with the governor, I was prepared to try out my limited Uzbek with him. Somewhat anxious from the tenseness of the moment, I extended my right hand and lifted my left hand, palm in, to my chest in the traditional Central Asian greeting.

"*Salaam Alekum,*" I said in Arabic. He responded in kind. I continued to grasp his hand and wished him good health and prosperity, speaking his language. His eyes brightened, and a dazzling smile creased his face. He graciously accepted my simplified Uzbek, and we exchanged several phrases. I again marveled at how speaking someone's mother tongue often opens the door to his or her heart. This was a good start. I soon discovered, however, that the dialect of Uzbek in northern Afghanistan and the one I studied in Tashkent and Termiz were quite different in pronunciation, verbal usage, and vocabulary.

We spoke with the governor about our desire to begin some new projects as God provided the staff and the funds. Afghans and other Muslim peoples don't find it at all strange to discuss plans with the added condition *"Inshallah"*—God willing. The authorities also addressed the lack of security in the area by reminding us that, since we were technically in a war zone, they couldn't guarantee our safety. This caution highlighted concerns for us but also underscored the value of our efforts to help those people displaced by the war.

As expected, the discussion covered other issues beyond security, such as our guest status as foreigners and followers of Jesus the Messiah. We explained to him that we were all committed Christians called there to serve as Christ commissioned us. We also stated that God would have us share our faith if others asked us, though we understood that our place as guests in their country meant that we could not expect or demand the attention of our hosts to our faith.

Feelings of understanding and unity were evident. They were careful not to offend us but wanted to emphasize how important it was to them that we continue to maintain our past history of service, for which they were grateful. We, in turn, offered our gratitude for their diplomacy and hospitality. By warning us not to push our Christian teachings, they preserved their role as defenders of their faith. And by allowing us to stay, they preserved their authority over us and secured our ongoing services to the community.

We left that meeting with the blessing to continue our much-needed work, as long as we didn't try to force our faith on the local people. We had not worn out our welcome. We could stay in northern Afghanistan and expand our work.

DESIGNATED DRIVER

After our meeting, we visited several boys' and girls' schools that we had built or repaired since the earthquakes. By this time, I began to appreciate someone who had been our constant companion since I met him at the landing strip in Feyzabad. His name is Halifa Hassamidin (*Halifa* means driver). We have since spent countless hours together in the car. He became one of my best Afghan friends and language tutors. He treated me graciously, even though he knew that I was struggling with his language. I sensed in him a genuine respect when he realized that I really wanted to learn from him.

My language lessons began immediately. I started asking a very useful question, *"In-chi-ast,"* which means "What is this?" Like a little kid, I continually pointed and asked. My new friend seemingly never tired of pronouncing the words and correcting my mimicking errors. Now, two years later, he is still patiently teaching and improving my broken Dari. He has become my favorite designated driver, and I enjoy our travels together. From the first day of our relationship, he has consistently found ways to assist me.

For the record, I don't drive in Afghanistan. I have a long list of reasons why, but several stand out. The first reason has to do with dignity. It's easy and tempting, when we live in another culture, to prove how much we Americans can do on our own. As a relief worker, I can fall into the trap of conveying to people that they need my help, but I don't need theirs. But I demean my Afghan friends if I communicate to them, "I'm going to help *you,* but there's nothing you can do for *me.*" If I engage in relief work with integrity, though, I'm going to encourage those I'm helping to do as much for themselves as possible. My goal is not to make them dependent on me. Instead, I want to assist them only until they can make it on their own. I encourage that, in part, when I depend on them for certain reciprocal favors. For instance, I honor Hassamidin's dignity when I ask him to drive for me.

Another reason I don't drive is reality. The people I'm trying to help know their land much better than I do. They even know when and how to ask for directions. They also need the work. The governments where we serve often worry about foreigners taking away gainful employment from their own citizens. They recognize that a foreigner may have special skills and resources their own people don't have, but driving is a good job for their citizens. In truth, I've had enough concerns in the last couple of years in Afghanistan that I'm truly grateful I haven't also had to worry about driving. Hassamidin helps keep me safe and sane.

A third reason I don't drive involves friendship and trust. Hassamidin knows my life is in his hands. He takes that responsibility seriously. In a culture that's very sensitive to shame, being entrusted with someone's life is a big deal. Also, spending all that time on the road has fostered a great friendship between us. In truth, I get a three-for-one deal: Hassamidin serves as my friend, my driver, and my language coach all at the same time. I surely would not speak as well, or have as much hair left, if I drove myself on the Afghan roads.

A BEND IN THE ROAD

DASHT-E QALEH—Since our scheduled time was quickly winding down, we left Rostaq and drove further northwest to Dasht-e Qaleh. I began to develop a real taste for the treacherous roads and the diet of dust we ate continuously.

Along the way, we stopped at the crest of a beautiful mountain pass. Hassamidin let us enjoy the view as he pointed out some of the geography of northern Afghanistan. Far to the north we saw Tajikistan. He pointed west and described Kondoz and Mazar-e Sharif, the areas under Taliban control. Later, we found out that while we were driving down the mountain toward Dasht-e Qaleh, the Taliban mounted a major assault on Taloqan, their next objective.

We made our first stop at the Shelter for Life office. I was in for several delightful surprises when I met the local staff. The engineer at our girls' school project was an Uzbek from Mazar-e Sharif. The cook that worked with him at the job site was an Uzbek from Rostaq. Then I learned that the other driver who works for us in this area is half Uzbek.

The Dasht-e Qaleh area population is 80 percent Uzbek. Of the two languages (Dari and Uzbek) I needed to manage, I already knew a fair amount of Uzbek. I was amazed to be in northern Afghanistan, surrounded by thousands of Uzbeks and a staff that spoke or understood Uzbek. I immediately felt at home.

We drove over to see the girls' school project that was almost complete. The community was grateful to our agency, not only for encouraging female education, but also for helping with the process. On the way, we received radio confirmation that Taloqan, General Massoud's stronghold, was falling into the hands of the Taliban. Their next target would probably be Khwojaghar and then the Tajik border area of Dasht-e Qaleh. Based on this news, it was obvious that hundreds of displaced people would soon be passing through our area as they fled the fighting in their home-towns.

With these rapid developments in mind, we met to talk about our response. So much for careful plans about long-term education and development—people in desperate need would be arriving soon. And that had to take priority.

At one point in the discussion, the regional director turned to me and said, "John, how would you feel if I left you here right now? We need someone from our international staff in Dasht-e Qaleh for at least the next few weeks. You could coordinate our emergency relief efforts for the refugees that will be arriving in the next few days."

I thought about the small bag I had brought, since this was supposed to only be a short visit. Suddenly I actually had a chance to stay. Considering this opportunity obviously meant an adjust-ment in my plans, because I had thought I was coming to teach and be involved in education. But conditions had changed. Was this the time for education or emergency assistance?

I love to teach. I also believe the axiom that says, "It's far better to teach a man to fish than to just give him fish." However, sometimes there's an unexpected bend in the road, and life turns complicated. If a man is starving, he may not be interested in my fishing lessons. Perhaps the teaching can wait until after I share some fish with him. Was this my opportunity to serve and help bring God's blessings to war-torn people? I remembered my vision in the Philippines and seeing myself serving the poor in Afghanistan. That wasn't a vision of teaching; it was a vision of service. Perhaps I was envisioning this very moment.

Concerned that I was hesitating, one of our local staff spoke up, "Please stay and help us, John."

I had actually already decided to stay, but their invitation ringing in my heart, spirit, and mind confirmed it. A seven-year dream finally came true that first week of September 2000. I chose to stay with my small bag of essentials and a conviction that "for such a time as this" God had ordained this mission of mercy inside Afghanistan. Simply said, I was in the right place at the right time.

With no luggage, no books, no computer, no shoes or winter clothes—nothing that I brought from the West—it took me only a minute to move into my new home. My housing featured the typical Afghan amenities: rugs and floor mattresses. I had no electricity, no running water, and no telephone . . . but lots of work to do.

Our regional director and another field officer, Chris Jones, crossed the border on the Amu Darya River at Ay Khanom that day. They headed back to Dushanbe after assuring me they would keep in touch. They also left me a limited budget to use for our emergency response. With a mixture of excitement and loneliness, I watched them cross the border. The encroaching sounds of warfare intruded on my solitude.

"Father God, thank you for bringing me here," I prayed. "Help

me to be your hands and feet to the people around me. Help me
never to forget your constant presence with me."

GETTING ORGANIZED TO SERVE

I knew I needed to recruit more help in order to handle the
incoming IDPs. The present staff in the office already had their
own responsibilities. As so often happens, my need was met in an
almost miraculous way.

A tall, gray-bearded, distinguished-looking fellow stopped by
our office during my first day on the job. I discovered he was
Engineer Massoud, who had worked with us during a 1999 shelter
program in Khvajeh Ghar. Shelter for Life had repaired hundreds of
homes under the direction of this skilled and caring associate. He
asked if we had more work. He knew the front line was moving
and wondered if we were going to help the IDPs who would soon
arrive. I hired him on the spot.

Once I settled into Dasht-e Qaleh, I lived as the locals lived. I
felt a little like a refugee myself. I slept on the floor in our office
most of the time. We actually had a small wood-frame bed with a
small mattress on it, but I preferred the floor where I could stretch
out. The staff and I ate together, worked together, and became
friends. None of them could speak much English, so it was a
language learner's heaven.

We had no time to waste. The refugees were coming. Massoud
and I drove to the local governor's office to talk about plans to help
IDPs. He was also Uzbek. We wanted to make arrangements for the
help of a bakery, in order to provide bread to the most vulnerable
refugees. They would need our help right away.

Afghan people enjoy a simple diet. They are not burdened with
many food choices. Rice, bread, tea, fruit, vegetables, yogurt, and a
lot of lamb make up their basic menu. As Muslims, they eat no
pork. Their daily bread is just that, bread—a flat loaf that looks like

large pita bread. They eat it every day, if they can get it. It also serves as edible silverware; ripped pieces of bread serve to scoop and sop up other foods. We knew that our first response to the needs of the IDPs would be to find a way to provide them with daily bread—both a necessity and a comfort.

Instead of discussing the bakery plan with us, though, Governor Nazar took us for a ride. Much to our surprise, he drove us to a place five miles outside the city on the Kowkcheh River. When the car stopped, my pulse quickened. Through the windshield, I could see a field covered with odd shelters, animals, bundles, tarps, and lots of people. It looked more like the ruins of a small town after a Texas tornado than a campsite. The governor figured there were about one hundred fifty families living under those makeshift tents that were handmade from blankets and rugs. The refugees were already here!

"These people need your bakery right now," he said. He had received word that morning that the first wave of displaced persons fleeing the Taliban attacks on Taloqan and Kondoz had crossed the river. They were setting up temporarily in this area of Dasht-e Qaleh just over the river from Khvajeh Ghar.

"I was about to send word of this to you when you appeared at my door," he said.

Engineer Massoud and I immediately began to survey and register the people at the campsite. As I'll explain later, this step is a crucial part of delivering help in an orderly way. Good assistance is usually the result of good survey and selection work. The next day we hired Hashim, a local baker, to make sixteen hundred loaves of bread daily for all these displaced families. We had an old Russian Jeep pickup truck to use for transporting the bread to the people.

Our original emergency response was simple but effective. Each day at the agreed hour, we stopped at the bakery and loaded the fresh loaves of bread. We hired Amrudin, a young lad from the Panjshir, to count the loaves of bread. He stacked them like pizza crusts in burlap bags and transported them out to the refugee camp. Then we distributed them to the families in exchange for the coupons we had issued during our survey. I'll never forget the joy, surprise, and gratefulness of those first eight hundred displaced people (one hundred fifty families) when they discovered that this foreigner and his staff were going to be able to give them bread every day. We became an unexpected answer to their unspoken prayers.

Unfortunately, that first bakery arrangement lasted only a few days. Our local baker simply couldn't handle the added business. His clay oven could only bake so many loaves an hour, and he wasn't prepared to work around the clock. That minor crisis was resolved by another miraculous circumstance.

Among the refugees were a baker and his family from Taloqan. Once we discovered this, we were able to help him quickly set up a bakery. His partnership with us preserved his own business and let him serve his poor neighbors in a practical and valuable way. Our daily work was developing under God's guidance.

THE PLACE OF MY DREAMS

I fell in love with DQ (Dasht-e Qaleh). Our wonderful Uzbek staff befriended me and made me feel at home. The DQ girls' school project (female education is something the Taliban hate), and our opportunity to respond quickly and compassionately to serve others appealed to my deepest desires. I had the daily privilege of feeding the hungry; exactly what Jesus Christ would do. I will always be glad I stayed. That decision has been confirmed many times over. I experienced joy and fulfillment in the place of my dreams, speaking Uzbek, learning Dari, and helping the poorest of the poor.

The Camp at Nowabad

NOWABAD—Before the Taliban or Al Qaeda exported their malicious hatred and evil acts of terrorism to the rest of the world, they practiced them for years in Afghanistan. In fact, during the last several years, humanitarian aid workers have frequently evacuated from northern Afghanistan because of the Taliban's savage treatment of anyone they perceived as an enemy.

For example, the first week of September 2000, the Taliban bombarded Taloqan, the capital of the Takhar province. Explosions and fires razed parks, orchards, and neighborhoods. Ten thousand families fled for their lives, but hundreds of civilians died, and the survivors experienced intense suffering. There, as in so many villages and towns of Afghanistan, destroyed homes collapsed on the innocent families within. Simple grave markers usually appeared in front of the rubble indicating to passersby that what remained of the house had become a tomb. No one in the family was left to dig out the bodies and give them a proper burial.

The Taliban's next target was Khvajeh Ghar, which they attacked around the middle of September, destroying 80 percent of the area. They massacred innocent civilians, planted hundreds of land mines, and booby-trapped empty houses. The village was instantly transformed into a ghost town. At least five thousand families barely escaped with only the clothes they were wearing and what they and their donkeys could carry.

Their appetite for mayhem unsatiated, the Taliban applied their own version of scorched-earth policy to the towns they overran, tossing incendiary devices on the roofs of homes and businesses. Plumes of smoke from smoldering villages blackened the air for days, like ominous low-hanging thunderclouds. Those who lived to tell of the atrocities knew they had no homes to which they could return.

Mud houses don't burn, but Afghan builders use wood timbers, woven mats, and straw-laced mud layers to roof their homes. Unfortunately, those materials blaze like tinder; fires catch quickly and consume the thatch, in turn igniting the heavier wood frames. The roof eventually collapses onto the rooms and families below. After the leaping flames die down, the glowing coals continue to burn until everything in the house is destroyed. After the embers cool, an eerie sight remains. Doors gone and windows empty, the skeleton houses resemble hollow-eyed Halloween masks, staring morosely into deserted streets.

Never looking back, the Taliban then set their sights on Dasht-e Qaleh. I had just moved into town. This area is strategic in the war effort, because it includes an important Tajik/Afghan border crossing on the Amu Darya River. The first bombs screamed into my neighborhood around September 20, 2000. We quickly stopped our work on the girls' school project, because our workers presented tempting targets to Taliban fighter pilots. Moreover, if the Northern Alliance lost this area, the school might be destroyed or used to house soldiers. In either case, it could not serve its intended purpose.

The fighting intensified as planes, tanks, and missiles daily shelled the town and villages of Dasht-e Qaleh. Those bombardments severely damaged several buildings along the main street. Within days we closed our office in DQ and moved everything up the mountain to Rostaq. Meanwhile, the courageous Northern

Alliance forces dug in and refused to budge in the face of the Taliban attacks.

All the other UN agencies and nongovernment organizations retreated from the front to their offices in Feyzabad. I spent nights in our Rostaq office but drove back down the mountain every day to the DQ area. People still in the danger zone desperately needed our assistance. But the daily, two-hour, bone-jarring ride each way began to wear me down because of the 120-degree heat and the thick, choking dust.

Once other agencies realized that we were determined to maintain a presence in the DQ area, they began asking us to manage their distributions too. The International Red Cross turned over to us hundreds of emergency response packets. The UN delivered loads of blue-plastic tarps to be used for shelters.

My days blurred into each other in a flurry of activity as I assigned workers to assist with the distributions, contacted other agencies for supplies, and planned for long-term needs such as provisions and preparations for the approaching winter months. We needed to find a place closer to Nowabad than Rostaq from which to operate.

MISSING!

Our original group of families, who had camped along the river, simply vanished one day. They had talked of moving if the battle-front showed any signs of breaking. More IDPs were passing through the area every day, and they brought late-breaking news of Taliban offensives.

One night a sizable Taliban raiding party tried to cross the river on horseback a little south of the campsite. They were spotted and ambushed by Northern Alliance Mujahidin. That report reminded me that front lines can be porous, and we could have unannounced hostile visitors at any time. The families at the river camp had obviously felt the same danger and moved.

When I drove out to the vacated site, I noticed how few signs indicated that almost a thousand people had lived there. Faint patterns on the ground distinguished foot traffic areas from where tents had stood. Here and there I could see worn circles where animals had been staked out. Deep ruts had been created by our pickup truck making its daily bread run.

I suddenly felt helpless. I couldn't tell if I was more upset because the camp was empty or because terrorized people had been forced to live there in the first place.

As I turned to leave, a movement on the far side of the river caught my eye. People and animals were approaching the water. I stood and watched a family cross the Kowkcheh River at a fording spot. The husband rode a donkey in front, sharing his saddle with a child. The bags hanging from his saddle dipped into the water as the overburdened animal trudged and splashed its way across. Behind him followed three or four horses loaded with packs. Each of the animals had a child perched among the bundles. A camel, carrying the wife and even more belongings, brought up the rear. I wondered what they had left behind as they hurriedly packed. Their little caravan plodded by me, still dripping, not stopping. Even the empty-eyed children stared straight ahead.

Later, I discovered that same little clan at a new, much larger encampment that formed just a few miles east of DQ in the village of Nowabad. Helpless and homeless families, who had been walking for days, reached a spot where the flatlands ended and the ground ahead rose steeply. They stopped, not because they finally felt safe, but because they knew the way onward was much more treacherous for their families.

CAMP TOUR

The most prominent feature of the Nowabad camp was the clump of three menacing tanks parked permanently on the spot where they had been gutted in some previous conflict. The barrel of one tank was aimed directly at a family's tent on the crest of a hill. It couldn't have missed. But it hadn't moved or fired a shell in years. Its long-deceased gunner hadn't moved the turret. It was dead in its massive tracks, literally. In truth, the hillside tent had been purposefully pitched, as if the family wanted to put themselves directly in the sights of the one thing they knew couldn't hurt them.

When I walked among the IDPs, I saw few wounds or injuries, but I did notice seas of shocked, vacant stares. These displaced people wandered into the camp carrying bundles of belongings, leading animals, and encouraging their children to take just a few more steps. The camp materialized in a location just far enough from the front to avoid Taliban rockets. As is often the case in a new camp, there was little obvious order, but the longer I watched, the more I realized that certain practical arrangements were being made.

From a distance, the encampment resembled an ocean of tents with fabrics of varied colors gently waving in the dusty breeze. This effect became more marked as we distributed bright blue tarps to supplement their flimsy tent coverings.

Walking among the people, however, I quickly realized that they were settling into family groups and leaving a certain amount of space between family sites. Fifty yards or more of open ground often marked the boundary between one family gathering and another. I have since learned that many of these people come from nomad stock, so they know how to camp. Even their lives at home don't differ all that much from the patterns they followed in the camp. But they had lost their homes and their means of support.

Under normal circumstances, many of these families would have traveled on foot or horseback, carrying basic camping gear in case they found themselves in a location with no family to offer them hospitality. This familiar experience became a hardship because they had left their homes under fire and didn't know when or if they would be allowed to return. Many believed they would find nothing left if they did return.

The open spaces in the camp kept it from feeling crowded. If I hadn't personally done the survey to register almost three thousand families, I would have doubted that so many people were in the camp. Their way of staking out areas made it difficult to see the entire camp at once, except from the air. That feature also offered a measure of protection. Taliban pilots seemed reluctant to drop bombs on the camp, because they couldn't hurt many people at one time.

The site had practically no vegetation. In fact, the color of the soil was desertlike, but the area featured sun-baked clay. Here and there were small mounds of earth that people put to use. On the leeward side of these small hills, families dug partial enclosures for their tents. Partly surrounded by soil, those tents were noticeably warmer during the chilly nights.

Using these natural humps in the ground, some families also created cooking areas and even mud ovens. The lack of natural shade anywhere caused many families to set up two shelters—one with sides close to the ground for warmth at night and the other with rolled-up sides to allow for shade and cooling breezes during the day.

Water for drinking, cooking, and tending livestock could only be found some distance from camp. The wells in the village itself had a limited supply. People had to walk a few miles to rivers and streams for water. People took turn watching small herds located roughly five miles to the north, where the Amu Darya river creates a wide swath of green through the parched lands of northern Afghanistan.

In spite of the extreme poverty all around us, I witnessed some amazing gestures of hospitality. Afghan culture strongly emphasizes the welcoming of strangers, so it was common to see families take in distant relatives or friends of the family. Local commanders and religious leaders even got involved, encouraging the area residents to house or help their displaced countrymen. However, due to the ethnic diversity that exists throughout Afghanistan, about three thousand families of the six thousand total IDP families that were forced to live in the open, did not have, at first, the good fortune of being "adopted" by local families.

BRINGING HOME THE BREAD

The maximum of eighteen hundred loaves of bread that our DQ bakery could produce daily would not feed the teeming thousands of families now in the area. Our bread supply effort, begun with the river camp, was almost immediately overwhelmed by the expanded needs of the larger camp at Nowabad. In meeting a short-term need, we had launched a new business, and that baker had plenty of customers even without our standing order.

So we needed a new plan. The average family in northeast Afghanistan includes at least five people. There are a lot of small families of widows and orphans but also many large families with ten or twelve children. Each person consumes an average of two to three loaves of bread per day. There was no quick fix for this crisis, and I was already thinking ahead to winter. As far as I knew, America had no plans to make food airdrops.

I immediately contacted USAID and the UN office in Feyzabad about the critical situation. If we couldn't actually bake the bread for the camp, perhaps we could provide enough wheat to each family to allow them to feed themselves. The agencies were eager to cooperate, especially if we took responsibility for distributing the resources. Within days, we began to supply wheat to the IDPs, provided by other countries, chiefly the United States.

PROVIDING THE POOR WANDERER SHELTER

The Office of Foreign Disaster Assistance (OFDA), a U.S. government agency that funds overseas emergency relief programs, also came through. They provided funds and challenged us not just to meet but to eliminate the humanitarian crisis in Nowabad. That became my task in the following months: to help shelter and feed these people. The goal was to keep them alive through the winter in hopes of eventually sending them home.

The Taliban had other plans. They intended for these Uzbek people to suffer and die as IDPs living in the open under rugs and blankets. To the Taliban, the IDPs were the wrong ethnic group and the wrong kind of Muslims. Though covered in religious trappings and expressed in the language of faith, the raw ethnic hatred and religious extremism of the Taliban demonstrated an evil and inhumane intent by finding joy in the suffering of others.

During those long and hectic days, my own role became clearer. I had a purpose to pursue for as long as I remained in Afghanistan. As a Shelter for Life representative, it was my privilege to respond as their stated purpose says: "quickly and compassionately to help those affected by wars, famines, and disasters." I sought to implement our vision to "provide the poor wanderer with shelter" (Isaiah 58:7 NIV). So I regularly prayed, asking God to give us wisdom and a way for us to serve these poorest of the poor.

My staff and I quickly decided to concentrate our relief work in the Nowabad area, because so many of the IDPs had settled there. Large concentrations of IDPs also made it to Rostaq and Feyzabad, but my immediate concern involved the Nowabad group. I sensed that the camp represented the last stop for many of the families; they had neither the strength nor willingness to trek on into the mountains. Whether or not the Taliban came, these people had decided they weren't going to run anymore.

AN ANSWER TO PRAYER

Our main project engineer, Massoud, began to look for a compound where we could store food and other relief materials, as well as provide some housing and work-space for our staff. This process was difficult for me, because Nowabad itself had become an "IDP town." Many families were already housing extra people.

I told Massoud, "We cannot make anyone leave their housing just to provide us a base of operations."

My first night in Nowabad I actually stayed in the house owned by Massoud's family. His relatives (ten people) and his family of eight squeezed even more tightly into their cramped quarters to offer me room and board. It was hard for me to eat, knowing that I was eating someone else's food, but they insisted on making me feel welcome. In fact, they would have been offended if I refused their hospitality. Entertaining guests is next to godliness for most Muslims. Central Asians believe in taking people in off the streets. Perhaps one of the reasons is that they know they may be the ones on the street when the Taliban comes to their town.

The main reason I stayed in Nowabad was personal survival. By the time the bombs fell in Dasht-e Qaleh, we had already started distributing food and relief on behalf of WFP, UN, International Red Cross, and other agencies in Nowabad. None of those agencies assigned staff to the area, but they did provide supplies. Every day we had to survey the needs of the people, identify new arrivals, and distribute wheat, blankets, clothes, plastic tarps, and other supplies among crowds of thousands. For me, doing this work while speaking an unfamiliar language (not one person among those thousands could speak English) was emotionally draining. I admit I didn't maintain a proper diet. By the end of each day, I was exhausted and reluctant to endure the abuse of the two-hour jostling ride back to Rostaq. It was easier, and I got more rest, by just staying in Nowabad.

We tried the daily commute for about ten days. At the time, I was not really aware of how close I came to a physical breakdown. The needs around me were so enormous and desperate that the extreme effort demanded of me seemed worth it. I wanted to help these families so badly. But by the second week, I knew I would not last long at that pace. The spirit may have been willing, but the flesh turned out to be predictably weak. My friend, Engineer Massoud, rescued me from my good intentions.

Massoud tried several times to find a place for me to live, but my concern that we not kick anyone out of their housing limited the options. Staying with his family didn't offer a long-term solution, although I deeply appreciated his concern for me.

As a Muslim and Christian working side by side, we often also prayed side by side. He heard me pray for our larger needs as an agency. We were stretched thin as an organization trying to function as a bridge between overwhelming needs and sometimes massive resources. And if the bridge broke, how would the help get through?

Living and working with Muslims hasn't necessarily taught me to pray without ceasing, but I can honestly say that I am now reminded to pray at least five times every day. I think, partly out of concern for me, Massoud began to target specific places in town. When we all prayed together, the staff often heard me speak personally to God, asking him to supply us with a place that included certain features. Meanwhile, my Muslim staff was busy with their own required prayers. I didn't realize Massoud was making mental notes of my conversations with God.

We needed a compound with at least four rooms, so that it was big enough for our growing staff. We also needed enough space to build a storage and distribution area. Some necessities, like wheat, we distributed directly from the transport trucks. We often delivered hundreds of fifty-kilogram bags in a single day. But we also received thousands of blankets and clothing packs, truckloads of tin sheeting, tons of beans and cooking oil, piles of wooden beams, and other items that we often had to store for several days. We tried to keep small quantities of other emergency supplies on hand too. We desperately needed storage space.

We also wanted permission to breach a wall in the compound for a gate big enough to use for truck deliveries. We had already been granted funding by USAID/OFDA (relief and development agencies of the United States government) to launch an emergency project to repair and build shelters and even assist local families as they took in IDP families. I knew I was praying for a compound with very special and unusual features, but it was what we needed; so I kept praying.

One day, Massoud took me to see a place owned by Alam. I was amazed. The walled compound had four rooms. The enclosed yard could accommodate two full basketball courts. That meant there was plenty of room to build a latrine (the compound had no bathroom), a work area, and two large storage/distribution centers. One wall offered an ideal location for a truck-sized gate. The enclosure already had a little outdoor kitchen that could be used to provide food for our busy staff.

As soon as I walked inside, I knew this compound exactly met our needs. God had answered our prayers in a big way, and it was obvious to everyone on our team. Even Alam was excited about the fact that God had led us to this property of his, where it could be used to help thousands of families.

When we set up shop, Nowabad had no running water, no electricity, no restaurants, no stores, not much of anything. It was little more than a small village of about three thousand families that suddenly doubled in population because of the IDPs. Eventually, the shelling of Dasht-e Qaleh forced the merchants from the bazaar to move up to Nowabad and set up shop on the outskirts of the refugee camp, but that didn't happen until later. We were hoping to improve both the immediate and long-term conditions in the village by coordinating relief and development from our new local office—the exact compound for which we had prayed and God had provided.

THE MOVE TO NOWABAD

We targeted October 1, 2000, as our moving day to Nowabad. Just before we set out from Rostaq, the skies opened and torrential rain forced us to take what we call "the river road." Many roads in Afghanistan are nothing but riverbeds. The sun dries and bakes them hard, and the rocks and gravel actually make them more dependable surfaces than the regular roads or trails.

When it's wet, the regular road from Rostaq to Nowabad is more like a mud toboggan run than a road. Once it's in that condition, it no longer offers a two-hour trip. In fact, the road becomes too dangerous to drive on at all. I've heard many stories of vehicles either getting stuck on the seven-thousand-foot-high mountainous pass or even sliding off the trail and tumbling thousands of feet down the mountainside.

Instead, we had to wind around the mountains on the river road for six interminable hours. We frequently had to climb out of the Jeep and match human horsepower to Afghan mire. Our move turned into a long, muddy epic saga.

When we finally arrived in Nowabad, it was already dark. We climbed out of our vehicles tired, wet, dirty, and without food or lights. We had little more with us than some bedding and blankets; our load for the trip consisted of only office supplies. We were relief workers badly in need of relief. It came in the form of our Afghan neighbors. They arrived with glowing lanterns, hot food, and a heartfelt welcome. That dark and damp moment was transformed by a simple act of generosity. God provides in humbling and overwhelming ways.

"Safe and Secure from All Alarms"?

More than the lack of comforts was the bigger issue of safety. I was repeatedly asked, "Is it safe to live in Nowabad?" I found it hard to describe a place as "secure" when you could stand on your roof and see the flares of war in the distance. At times I didn't want to talk on our CB-like radio because others might be frightened to hear the sounds of combat in the background. Continual

My first job: Giving daily bread to the displaced in Desht-e Qaleh
(September 11, 2000)

Beside Engineer Massoud with our staff in Nowabad
(October 2000)

Wheat from America blesses the war-torn people of Afghanistan
(November 2000—Nowabad Camp)

*Blessing the
bewildered in
Rostaq with
blankets,
a sleeping kit
and soap*
(Winter 2000–2001)

Our dedicated supervisor, Khalidjon, distributes sandalees, blankets, and soap
(Winter 2000–2001)

Writing reports/letters and journaling
(Rostaq office, Christmas 2000)

*With our trusted accountant/office manager, Mahboob, and
faithful driver of four years, Hasan*

*Preparing for wheat distribution for our Host Family Project in the thirteen
villages of Dasht-e Qaleh*

On the road to the border at Eshkashem (January 2001)

Giving wheat, oil, and sweaters to female students at the school in ChaAb (Spring 2001)

With our skilled carpenter, Akbar, and his assistant
(Spring 2001; school construction)

"The first day you meet, you are friends.
The next day you meet, you are brothers."
—Afghan Proverb

Samaritan's Purse—the American children affected by 9/11 reach out to the children of Afghanistan (Christmas 2001)

Unloading bags of USAID wheat at our storage and distribution center

Surveying in Mawmaii (village featured on CNN)
where we are building a school for boys and girls

The infamous river crossing on an Afghan raft (Spring 2002)

reminders kept us from ever taking the war for granted, even on the quiet days.

On my way into the camp area each morning, for instance, I passed by two Northern Alliance mobile rocket launchers. With their massive barrels aimed west, they appeared less menacing in the light than when their missiles ignited and shot from their fifteen-foot long tubes during the night.

When launches were conducted by day, the ground throughout the camp shook from the jolting recoil as the missiles departed. The sound always got my attention, day or night. It wasn't the sudden "whomp" or crack of artillery fire. A few seconds of ignition and warm-up preceded the launch, followed by the metallic hiss of the missile leaping from the tube and roaring into the sky. Seconds later, the missile would land with a dull echo on the far side of the Kowkcheh River. After a while, I realized that the ground where I was standing was still quivering when the missiles' arrival rocked the ground along the Taliban front line.

The cemetery outside Nowabad often caught my eye during my rounds. I could see it on my way to camp. Fresh mounds marking new graves appeared frequently. The Afghan flags flying from short poles on most of these graves indicate a war-related death. Life after life, violently snuffed out. I couldn't help but wonder what it must have been like in my own country during the Civil War, as thousands of Americans killed each other. War is horrible and heart wrenching, even more so when you're living in the midst of it. Yet, despite the horror around me, I was thankful that God was allowing me to be in this place at this time "to give the poor wanderer shelter."

During these months, I had staff from other organizations say, "John, you're crazy to live there and work so close to the front line." I assured them I wasn't a danger junkie. I was just trying to walk a fine line between reasonable caution and obedience. I remain convinced that Jesus would make time for these needy ones, if he were physically still here on earth.

PASSING IT ON

The move to Nowabad transformed us into a major participant in relief efforts in that part of northern Afghanistan. Since September 2000, I've had the privilege of managing dozens of large distributions. Many of these involved such quantities of food and materials and such large numbers of IDPs that the distributions took several days or weeks to carry out. The following list represents only part of the items we were privileged to present to needy people:

- WFP (World Food Programme): Over four thousand tons of wheat and five thousand gallons of cooking oil for both emergency and food-for-work projects.
- UNOCHA (UN Office for Coordination of Humanitarian Affairs): hundreds of bundles of blankets and plastic tarps for temporary shelter.
- ICRC (International Committee of the Red Cross): thousands of basic emergency kits with blankets, a cooking pot, soap, and plastic sheeting.
- OFDA (Office of Foreign Disaster Assistance): tons of beans, over fifty thousand liters of cooking oil, and thousands of blankets—all procured and transported from Tajikistan; pile after pile of wooden beams and bamboo mats for shelter repairs; firewood and sheets of tin for a woodstove-making project.
- Over seven thousand sorted bags of clothes and sleeping kits from various charitable organizations in the U.S. and Europe.
- Some thirty thousand Samaritan's Purse Operation Christmas Child shoe boxes full of toys and school supplies for children.

These relief efforts had their exciting moments. In fact, the logistics involved in delivering help to people fascinate me. And now that I have participated in the process, I realize what a crucial role people play who are on the front lines of relief, making sure the assistance that's generously provided actually gets to those for whom it is intended. This isn't always easy in Afghanistan, as you will see.

Dangerous Duty

NOWABAD—Even though the help we were able to provide was good for the people in Afghanistan, delivering it to them was often challenging. In fact, it was sometimes quite dangerous. The war, drought, hunger, and extreme need created desperate conditions. On rare occasions, I was even targeted.

For every sack of wheat or container of cooking oil we gave to a displaced person, as much as an hour of preparation had already been invested in it. Careful groundwork prevents a distribution from becoming a riot. I was taught this premise well, and I've confirmed the wisdom of it by my mistakes.

Distribution groundwork begins with a survey. In the case of an IDP camp, every family must be carefully interviewed. Information about family size and their specific needs allows a relief agency to more effectively provide supplies and to organize the distribution. The personal interview equips us to treat them as real people, rather than just a set of needs. In the course of these conversations, we often discover valuable skills in the camp. The family of bakers we were able to help get back into business, for instance, was identified in our initial survey of the river camp group.

In exchange for registering for help, families receive coupons to exchange for goods at the distributions. This eliminates the temptation for them to go through the distribution line more than once to stock up on supplies. No coupon? Sorry, no benefit. When a camp numbers in the thousands, the staff could never remember who has or hasn't already been through the line.

Supply agencies like the UN used our surveys and registration lists as the basis for their allotments to the camp. Without that data, our guesses about how much wheat and other items were needed would have been grossly inaccurate.

For instance, the Nowabad camp was deceptively spread out. At its greatest size, an observer would never have guessed that three thousand nomadic families were living in the shelters scattered over the plains. In fact, our survey uncovered twice as many displaced people living in the area than we could account for in the camp itself, because so many village families had given shelter to refugees in their homes.

Needless to say, the work and hours required to both prepare for and actually carry out ongoing distributions was overwhelming to my staff and me. We were drowning in a tidal wave of homeless, desperate people pushed to the brink of disaster by the merciless Taliban.

LOVING AN ENEMY

I first met Daud in a crowd of several thousand hungry people at the Nowabad camp. I was with our staff distributing wheat. We might just as well have been handing out bags of gold in the eyes of the people. Wheat is precious in Afghanistan, because bread is made from it. Afghans spend part of every day preparing it. Bread in Afghanistan represents life, and it is often treated as a holy substance. Our most appreciated distributions have always been either wheat or wheat flour, most of which comes from USAID.

I had no idea that Daud instantly declared me an enemy when he learned that I was a Christian. Since I had been in the area for less than a month, few people really knew me yet. I had spent most of my time with my staff and those first one hundred fifty families we were helping in Dasht-e Qaleh. But we had just moved to Nowabad.

At that point, the Nowabad Camp held more than a thousand families (some five thousand people) and was still growing. They all knew that I was not Uzbek, because I spoke with an accent. They had also concluded I was not Tajik/Afghan, because I could only spit out a few words in Dari or Tajik. Those who listened to others call me by name knew me as "Mr. John," who had come to help them. Those who were curious and asked my staff learned that I am not a follower of their prophet Mohammed but of Jesus Christ, the Messiah.

The first time I noticed Daud, he was making his way through the crowd with his fingers in the shape of a cross. He was trying to turn the crowd against me. He kept shouting, *"Qafir! Qafir!"* which means "infidel" or "unbeliever." He was using the cross shape to label me as a Christian.

Daud had a fairly common distortion of Christian theology that promotes rejection. Muslims are often taught that the Christian doctrine of the Trinity means that God had a wife named Mary, and they together had a son named Jesus. This is why some Muslims refer to Christians as unbelievers, infidels, or idolaters. I would have liked to explain to Daud that the concept of God's having a wife is just as blasphemous to me as it is to Muslims, but I didn't get a chance.

Daud's efforts to provoke a riot failed; people in the crowd had little interest in a theological discussion. While he was busy stirring the pot of hatred, we were busy handing out bread in the name of love. The consistent compassion of our work spoke louder than the fact that I represented another way of life or belief. Many of them probably didn't care if I ate pork, watched movies, or prayed to God by saying, "Our Heavenly Father." With hungry bellies, it gladdened their hearts to receive bread from this *Qafir*. They weren't about to argue over the accuracy of Daud's accusations. I was simply a friend in their time of need; so, in their minds, I must be a friend indeed. Besides, none of their Muslim brothers from other countries were helping them. In fact, the Taliban were seeking to destroy them in the name of Allah or Islam. Those on the receiving end of Muslim-against-Muslim violence make an excellent point: Something is distorted in the picture of Afghanistan.

Daud pushed through the crowd trying to get to me on two different occasions, but he was headed off by my staff or some other good Samaritan. However, he was determined and didn't give up easily. Those I questioned later said they could see it in his eyes— the hatred and disgust, and the desire to harm me. He was evidently oblivious to the consequences. He could only see what he *thought* I represented.

Finally, his chance came when I jumped off the truck from which we were distributing some twenty-five hundred bags of wheat. As I landed on the ground, the crowd parted, both for their own safety and also out of respect for the guest in their country who had come to help them.

Just as I caught my balance and straightened up, Daud rushed me with an iron rod. He moved so suddenly that no one was quick enough to stop him. I had no time to think about how to respond.

As he raised the rod to hit me between the eyes, I said, *"Isa Masih nomidan borib keting!"* A rough translation from Uzbek would be, "In the name of Jesus, get out of here!"

Stunned, he immediately stopped and just stood there. Engineer Massoud quickly shoved me to the side in the direction of our Hilax pickup. The sequence unfolded like an old-fashioned movie, in which Halifa Habib (our half-Uzbek getaway driver) knew trouble was coming and was ready to help me make a quick escape.

The next day, Daud showed up again, empty-handed, to apologize. Several days later, he actually assisted us in one of the distributions. Now, instead of stirring up the crowd as he had previously done, he wanted to help with crowd control.

This episode taught me several lessons. I was able to show forgiveness to this man who threatened my life. I also witnessed the powerful effects such forgiveness has on others. Daud seemed to conclude, *I would be a fool to kill Mr. John. In fact, instead of him needing to be more like me, I need to be more like him.* I realize, in that set of circumstances, that I did very little and God did a lot. Even my verbal response to Daud's attack simply came as an instant, helpless dependence on God, not some bold, well-developed plan on my part.

In my daily interactions with humble, thoughtful Muslims, I find that we agree on many important principles. God is good. Evil always bows before good. And the only way to overcome evil is with good. By God's mercy our lives can show something winsome, holy, and humble. Our actions can be life-giving and loving. The truth of the gospel message is difficult to reject when it comes wrapped in an attitude of compassion, mercy, and service. I see this premise at work on a very practical level in Afghanistan. As people get to know me personally, misconceptions and stereotypes about Christians often vanish.

I have occasionally been surprised at the approaches my local defenders have taken. One newcomer decided to publicly challenge me by asking what business a foreigner had being there since I wasn't even Muslim. Before I could answer, one of the wise old men in town stepped forward for attention. The buzz of the crowd stilled. He turned to the accuser and said, "Mr. John is a better Muslim than all of us."

My initial flush of gratefulness that someone of his stature would defend me in public paled before the unexpected honor wrapped in his compliment. He explained my efforts in Muslim terms. His response meant, at least in part, that Mr. John lives his life the way we're supposed to live our lives as Muslims, submitted to God. His kind words renewed my own determination to try harder to live that way.

MR. ANGRY TURBAN

Not long after the episode with Daud, I encountered an interesting old man I call Mr. Angry Turban. Again, we were in Nowabad camp, which had now grown to more than fifteen thousand people. We had not registered them all yet, and we were well beyond our capacity to assist them all at one time. We had seven trucks of wheat to distribute, and people were still struggling to learn that this wasn't a first-come-first-served operation.

The system of registering people and giving them coupons for wheat works very well *once it's in place*. But it takes time to interview each family and assess their needs. Still, the process has a calming effect on the huge crowds. People know, once they have their coupons, they *will* receive wheat. And the coupons allow us to gauge the size that the distributions will be.

There's nothing so terrifying, however, as facing a crowd of hungry people who can clearly see that you have no way of physically stopping them from rushing the piles of wheat bags on the trucks. Desperate people can easily jump to the wrong conclusion that some people might get an unfair share while they might not get any. Others just get tired of waiting their turn. So many things can turn a peaceful crowd into an angry mob.

I had never seen Mr. Angry Turban before. He must have been in the crowd for quite a while before he figured out that, since he hadn't registered, he wasn't likely to receive wheat that day. He realized he would have to give up his place in line to find one of our staff and get directions for registration. So he became upset. He unwound the turban from his head and began to whip the thick rope of cloth overhead and then slam it on the ground, all the while shouting his frustrations at the top of his voice.

Every time he hit the ground, a cloud of dust puffed up around him. Truthfully, he was expressing what a lot of other people were also feeling. So the crowd responded with restlessness. Some shouted agreement and encouragement to him. I could see we were about to lose control of the crowd. Actually, I had a certain amount of frustration myself that day, and getting down in the dust to have it out with him almost seemed like a good idea. I felt helpless and alone. I really didn't know what to do, so I lifted my eyes and hands toward heaven in desperate prayer for help.

To my amazement, the cavalry arrived in the form of the local governor. He made me a believer in God-ordained human authority that day. I watched as he literally took physical control of the situation. He waded into the crowd swinging a short stick around his head. He wasn't trying to hurt anyone, but his actions definitely cleared a path through the unrest and got people refocused on the task at hand. Once he had the crowd's attention, he berated them for several minutes. He scolded their lack of patience and their disrespect for people who were only there to help them. I saw how powerful a tool shame could be when used with compassion.

Eventually Mr. Angry Turban and his friends all received wheat. And several days later, he came up to me in the camp shouting, "Mr. John! Thank you, Mr. John!" Then he slowly approached me and humbly stroked my beard with his callused hands—a gesture that conveys great honor and respect in Central Asia. He had come to understand that I was on his side, and he was expressing his gratitude for my help. As I accepted his thanks, I wished I could tell him that I had been feeling the same way he did that day. That incident remains indelibly etched in my mind.

THE SLUGGER

These dangerous and tense distribution times had their way of bringing out the worst in me too. Sometimes I would get angry with the people's pushing, complaining, and general lack of appreciation for the supplies. And sometimes I let people know that I was upset. I'm sure that anger worked at times for my safety, but I disliked the feelings. After such reactions, I always went back to apologize, and each time I was welcomed and well received. They often responded with apologies in return, saying, "You were right to treat us that way, because we were trying to take advantage of the situation."

One of these occasions happened when a great crowd of hungry and angry people showed up outside our compound door. They had decided that we were hoarding food inside and were determined to "crack open the storehouse." Snarling in their intentions, they sounded like a pack of starving, savage wolves now in sight of some sleeping sheep.

Hunger motivates. I've seen its powerful effects on a tormented father or mother, who has to watch a child die of malnutrition. I've seen its greedy look in people's eyes when the pile of wheat shrinks, and they realize that there may not be any left when their turn comes. Their desperation can quickly turn savage.

On that particular day, the crowd in front of our house started getting out of hand. They pounded on the gates, shouting a chorus of demands. Some of them threatened our staff with physical harm. Others were trying to climb inside over the seven-foot-high mud walls.

I glanced around our compound. If we swung open the gates, mayhem would surely follow. We had a small quantity of wheat and some other basics that we kept on hand for critical emergencies. Those would disappear in moments, of course. Then their disappointment that we could provide no more would quickly turn to rage. A mob never thinks twice about cutting off the hand that may be able to feed it tomorrow.

I don't know whether I reacted in anger, righteous indignation, or simply to save our lives. I applied the lesson I had learned from the governor as I watched him control a crowd. I grabbed a piece of wood about the size of a walking stick and went to clean house. I think I held the wood like the Louisville Slugger bat I used to play baseball with as a kid.

I flung open the gate and began to swing this stick of wood over my head, banging it hard on the ground after each step. I roared a wild mixture of Uzbek, Dari, English, Spanish, and Russian that made up in intensity for what it lacked in meaning. I didn't froth at the mouth, but only because it was too dry. I'm sure I sounded unhinged. Thankfully, I didn't kill or hurt anyone, since I had never practiced this approach before. But as I moved forward, the crowd parted like the Red Sea. They also became very calm and quiet. I think they were probably more shocked than impressed.

As a result of my demonstration of baseball and shouting skills, I suddenly had a silent, captive audience. I told them that we were doing the best we could with the staff we had. The bad weather delayed many of our supplies. Entire truck convoys often got stuck or stranded in the mud. The complications of war didn't help either. The border crossing closed from time to time, making fuel for our trucks scarce and our imported materials nonreceivable. I even took another cue from the governor and applied a little shame to the situation. If they really thought we were hoarding supplies, then they should appoint two or three representatives to come into the compound with me and verify that our larder was empty. They were not acting with honor in accusing us of wrongdoing they couldn't prove. I told them we were sorry we couldn't help their hunger that day, but their anger wasn't going to make things better.

They nodded with a sense of understanding. Calm settled over the crowd, like a raging storm returning to peaceful silence. Many of the older men began to say, "Mr. John is right." They looked at me slyly, as if to add an unspoken, *Mr. John is crazy too.* We then began to talk about better methods for future distributions and more trust that our plans always had their benefit in mind.

CONFRONTATION

One of the largest World Food Programme distributions I implemented involved over forty big trucks loaded down with double rations of wheat for forty-five hundred families. Winter was coming, and the WFP thought they might not be able to deliver anything else for a month or two. So each family was scheduled to receive one hundred kilograms of wheat, which meant transporting nine thousand sacks weighing a total of 450,000 kg. Bad weather, mud slinging, lack of fuel, and repeated truck breakdowns turned the distribution into a three-week ordeal.

During one bout of snow, rain, and mud, we waited seven days for trucks to arrive. By the time we heard the radio announce that the trucks were approaching, I was more than eager to start, and so were thousands of people.

During a typical distribution, we read off the registration list, checked their cards, and gave out the wheat. The assembly line format works well. But the larger picture just shows an open field with thousands of people milling around. A casual observer might conclude that they were looking at mass chaos, but we knew this chaos had some order.

I really felt at home in these settings. At times the mood of the crowd even turned festive. We were participating in something good. Our beneficiaries were becoming our friends. I could speak their language and loved sharing my life with them. I knew I was sent to serve them and was enjoying it, despite the obstacles and difficulties.

Sometimes I got so caught up in the work that I wasn't aware of what was going on around me. This huge distribution had me so involved at the wheat truck that I failed to notice a man trying to disrupt things. Later I learned that he was a local commander named Dusti. He was telling my staff at the table (the ones reading the list) to stop the distribution. He claimed that he had specific orders from the main commander. Their intended plan was to confiscate a certain amount of the wheat for "military purposes." After he and his men took their allotment, he said the distribution could resume.

These incidents happen sometimes in Afghanistan. Many local commanders rule out of fear. What they say goes, whether good or bad. If they don't think they or their families get what they deserve or want, they may steal from others, because they have the power to do so.

In fact, on one particular occasion an International Red Cross distribution in our area got so out of control that the local commanders stole over 70 percent of the resources. The disaster occurred on a day that my staff and I were not around to help. We had asked ICRC to wait one day so we could help, but they had their own schedule and agenda. They arrived with lots of goodwill and supplies, but they lacked three crucial components for effective distribution of relief:

1. favor and relationships with local people,
2. friends in high places, and
3. a track record of trustworthiness in the area.

Their lack of forethought was bluntly rewarded. They were treated as foolish strangers, and their supplies were looted.

Thankfully, during this World Food Programme distribution, our plans weren't similarly thwarted. When Dusti announced his intentions to confiscate a portion of our wheat, one of my staff finally came to tell me what was happening. I knew immediately something was fishy, because the main Uzbek commander, Mawmir Hasan, was very supportive of our work. In fact, I'm glad to call him a friend. He had already told me that if anyone caused a problem to let him know. Frankly, I didn't have time for the interruption that day. So, in righteous anger, and determined to not let this spirit of fear win the day, I began to run in the direction of this man, grabbing a cane from an old man on the way. I applied my stick-swinging technique again to chase him away. Fortunately, it worked again.

In fact, this technique worked so well that I'm glad I had to use it only a few times. I'm afraid I would have eventually hurt somebody, likely me. On this occasion, the crowd cheered. They were impressed and grateful. Later, I heard some of them referring to me as the "guy who fears only God."

Thinking back on these confrontations, I can't say that my actions or reactions were always appropriate. But I'm convinced that I could have done much worse if I had *failed* to act. Fear can be a snare and a powerful tool in the hand of one's enemy.

One phrase that I use often now is *"Fakat Khudo-dan korkaman,"* which in Uzbek means, "I only fear God." I want to live that way. And neither my Muslim nor my Christian friends have any problem with that approach to life.

CROSSING THE FRONT LINE

Only a few times did I actually cross the river that defined the front line. Most of our staff kept a personal buffer zone of several miles between them and the river. Among the IDPs, however, people forded the river almost daily, traveling both directions. Many of them, even those living in areas taking fire from both sides of the conflict, were either unwilling or unable to leave. Most believed that their homes would be looted if they fled to safety; they watched it happen to their neighbors' homes every day.

Word of our life-saving distributions traveled across the river, and I began to receive appeals for help from those destitute people too. A small delegation from the village of Mawmaii showed up on my doorstep with a list of seventy families in desperate need. I knew of this village. It was already infamous as the site of bloody massacres and atrocities by the Taliban. That "go where no one has gone before" part of me instantly wanted to take help across the river.

When I worked out the math in my head, I realized I couldn't handle seventy fifty-kilogram bags of wheat by myself. I had to recruit help for this dangerous trip. Since I had no authority to order any of our staff into harm's way, I sat down to evaluate the benefits and risks of the operation. These were families we only knew through others. Could this invitation to help actually be a trap? Would we be caught in crossfire? Were the risks to life and limb justified, if three hundred fifty people received life-preserving help? Did an effort like this go beyond the boundaries of my role as a relief worker? Were my internal compulsions a good enough reason to embark on this mission?

I tried to consider these questions seriously. Other potential liabilities also came to mind. We couldn't take a vehicle across the river because the bridges were gone. We would have to transport the wheat and ourselves over the surly water by raft. Afghans have a creative version of a raft that they use in rural areas. A small passenger platform rests atop several sewn-together, inflated cowhides. The homemade design doesn't exactly inspire confidence. Leaving the vehicle also meant leaving behind the Codan radio. So once we crossed the river, we would have to remain out of touch until we returned.

I called Supervisor Jafar, who was displaced from an area near Mawmaii, into my office and laid all these questions and concerns on the table. I chose him because of his personality and familiarity with the region. He listened quietly. When I was finished, I asked, "Will you go with me?"

He sat there for a moment, brow furrowed, looking at something distant through the window. Then he met my eyes, and his face slowly creased into a smile.

"Yes, Mr. John. I go with you," he carefully pronounced in his simple English.

I can't decide which experience I value more—the joy of helping people or the camaraderie of doing it with others. For Jafar this was an invitation to help some of his own neighbors. For me it was another open door to serve a war-torn people.

After all the worry, the trip itself turned out to be routine. The multiple trips ferrying wheat across the river went without a single dunk in the water. Villagers showed up to help us carry the sacks away from the river to a distribution point near the village. Everyone participated in glad, grateful, and cooperative ways. There was a spirit of sharing, since we couldn't transport enough for everyone. Those on our list readily shared their wheat with hundreds of other families still surviving in this devastated area. How sweet it was to offer some help to those who had seen their innocent loved ones brutally killed by the Taliban.

This village of Mawmaii soon gained worldwide attention as a result of the two-part report done for CNN by Saira Shah— "Beneath the Veil" and "Unholy War." We were able to assist her during both her visits to the area. As a result of that exposure, there will soon be a school in Mawmaii to offer education to the children who have suffered so much. My companion, Jafar, and I turned out to be only the first of many who have gone to Mawmaii with humanitarian aid.

UNDER FIRE

Another dangerous day occurred at Lolamaidon, a place that doesn't appear on any maps. We were there giving out beans, chickpeas, and cooking oil to needy families right on the front line. The location turned out to be a beautiful area at the foot of some mountains, with the Kowkcheh River flowing in the valley close behind us. We were in no-man's-land on the wrong side of the river.

Trees shaded our work, and hundreds of little children came to us. The sounds of people talking and children laughing made me forget the war for a little while. I felt the sheer goodness of what we were doing wash over me. Who I was didn't matter. I'm sure not one of them guessed that I was an American. All of these people thought I was from Turkey, or Uzbekistan, or some other neighboring country. They didn't care who I was; they were just grateful someone had come to help.

During the distribution, fighting broke out on the front line. Gunfire shattered the peaceful moment, and the shots were much too close for my comfort. Taliban jets flew low overhead, and our little crowd vanished. I confess that this suddenly turned into an exciting day for me. But my staff, who have lived in a vicious hellhole for decades of war, weren't enthused. We quickly packed up what supplies we had left and sped back towards Nowabad.

As we approached Dasht-e Qaleh, we saw General Massoud's vehicle on the road. We stopped to make the appropriate greetings to show our respect. Then, as he drove off, a Taliban jet circled again. I'm certainly no military strategist, but it appeared to me that they were trying to take the Lion of the Northern Alliance out of the picture. He really represented everything that was keeping the Taliban from taking control of the entire country. General Massoud was fearlessly holding on to his stronghold in the north. For Afghanistan, he was truly the minister of defense. Without him, my life would have been in a lot more danger.

A Channel of Blessings

NOWABAD—Even under the best circumstances, refugee camps don't replace homes. Camps can serve to provide emergency housing and even help people to survive, but they're not intended to be permanent. Still, refugee camps present very strong images to potential donors; they touch people's heartstrings because the needs seem so staggeringly apparent. Refugee camps offer great "photo ops." But the best day at a refugee camp isn't the day the big-name film crew arrives or even the day the trucks of wheat rumble through the gates. The best day of all is when the camp closes, because no one is left inside. Everyone has gone home.

I've had to learn some painful lessons about where real needs are during my last two years in Central Asia. Needs aren't always obvious, nor are they always found where you might expect. The conditions inside a barbed-wire enclosure of blue plastic survival tents may actually be better than those in a dusty village of mud huts nearby.

Why? A managed camp will probably have a primitive-but-effective hygiene system. Many villages in Afghanistan don't have even a single latrine for hundreds of people. Relief agencies may haul in truckloads of safe water, or they may even sink a shallow well, while a few miles down the road, people in their homes are drinking polluted river water. A local farmer may pass people from the camp carrying free sacks of wheat as he slowly trudges to his fields where he has to watch his precious crops wither in the glaring sun.

THE HIDDEN CRISIS

When the large camp formed outside of Nowabad, we supplied wheat and other emergency relief to the displaced people. We were certainly a more dependable source than they expected, given the problems created by the war and the drought. But the living situations in the village of Nowabad itself were as desperate as the conditions in the camp. People had homes, but they didn't have food. Many families had taken in relatives who were IDPs, causing even more hardship. Village systems that could barely handle the basics of ordinary life suddenly experienced the pressure of a highly increased population. The absence of any plumbing or latrines in Nowabad meant that hygiene quickly became a major problem. Human waste, which normally was left on the ground for dogs, began to accumulate to hazardous levels. The few wells in town couldn't begin to keep up with the demand for water by a doubled population.

Persistent drought made it hard for the local farmers to survive. The war made many products scarce, even for those who did have money. War causes chaos in a country, even miles from the front lines. Those who provide effective relief and development in a crisis are not just those who move swiftly. Wisdom sees the real needs and finds a way to meet them.

When I walked into the bakery in Dasht-e Qaleh with money and arranged for the delivery of sixteen hundred loaves of daily bread, I cornered the local market, in order to meet the needs of the IDPs that had just fled Takhar and Kondoz. I unwittingly pushed the baker into a conflict of interests. Should he try to meet his new largest-paying customer's (me) demands, or should he continue to serve his long-time customers, who would still be buying their bread from him long after the camp was just a bad memory? My attempt to meet one real need created another potential problem.

This bread predicament is just one example of unintended issues that spring up when the need is greater than the supply. By providing bread to the displaced families in the camp, I unintentionally and unknowingly created a bread shortage for the citizens of Dasht-e Qaleh. Fortunately, this was resolved in a few days by setting up the bakery in the camp with a displaced baker. That turned out to be a practical and providential solution. Other challenges were not so easy to meet, though. The very existence of the IDP camps tortured me every day.

As we at Shelter for Life discussed what we were learning about responding to various kinds of crises, we realized we had made some significant discoveries. The situation inside Afghanistan was a unique and painful classroom, because it combined some of the worst possible scenarios of disaster. War, earthquakes, floods, and drought were all occurring at the same time. One catastrophe had piled onto another. If an entire nation today could identify with the experience of desolation and loss described in the Book of Job in the Bible, that nation would be Afghanistan.

THE HOST FAMILY PROJECT

We were convinced that we could develop other ways to approach this huge humanitarian need than simply establishing and servicing refugee camps. In conditions like these, families suffer. They die of hunger, cold, sickness, or just plain hopelessness. In the first few months I was there, we devised a plan to respond to the general needs that were larger than the camp. In fact, we did everything we could to *empty* the camp.

We channeled our energy, expertise, and efforts toward eliminating a potential open-air graveyard of displaced victims. Even while the war and the drought continued, we reduced the camp at Nowabad from an all-time high of three thousand families (fifteen thousand people) to about three hundred families. That amazing result allowed us to say that, while there were still pressing humanitarian needs, there was no longer a humanitarian crisis for the IDP or local community of the Dasht-e Qaleh area.

Afghan/Muslim culture provided one of the key insights to the plan that we called the Host Family Project. Our approach also developed as we prayed and thought about the differences implied by our dual name—Shelter Now and Shelter for Life. We wanted to be effective in our relief efforts, as well as constructive in our development work. We wanted to provide immediate help in times of crisis while operating with an awareness of long-term needs. In a sense, we tried to answer this question: If the world community is willing to contribute a certain amount of money and supplies to respond to a crisis in a particular area, are there better ways to use those funds and provisions than by creating and maintaining refugee camps? Our answer to that question was the Host Family Project.

The people in Nowabad, as part of their culture, religious belief, and sense of duty to extended family, were already taking in displaced relatives or family friends when the camp sprang up on the edge of town. The village population swelled too. At one point, there were as many IDPs staying in homes in the village as in the huge makeshift camp. Our move to Nowabad was very difficult, because we didn't want to displace people again. The local systems were stretched to the breaking point. The "hidden" crisis in the village was partially created because the resources coming into the area were going almost exclusively to the people in the camp.

Camps present relief workers with a captive audience. That population doesn't require the effort that goes into extensive community surveys or the time involved in all the preparatory work. Camps level the playing field to misery's lowest common denominator.

In contrast, small towns form complex social systems. Surveying the displaced that are dispersed in village housing presents relief agencies with logistical nightmares. Family problems are not as noticeable and people are less accessible than those who live in organized tents. Needs vary greatly. Sometimes the complicated survey process is traded in for rough estimates and ineffective use of resources.

But what would happen, we wondered, *if we empowered the people in the village to take in and provide shelter for people in the camps? What if, instead of paying for flimsy tents and tarps out in the open, we used the same money to help people in the village construct added rooms to their homes, build permanent latrines in their family compounds, and provide food for all of them?* In exchange, these families would shelter the IDPs until they could return to their own homes. What would happen if, instead of maintaining a camp, we spent the same money to vastly improve the infrastructure of an entire community?

The Host Family Project was the kind of success that still brings me to tears. Our approach and hard work paid off. The incentives we gave to the local community indeed encouraged and enabled them to provide sustained assistance to their displaced countrymen. This combined effort impacted almost everyone in DQ. It did much more lasting good than the camp.

I'll never forget the day I looked over what had been the sprawling camp at Nowabad and realized that it was almost empty. I wept for joy. By then, we had helped families in the village build over a thousand additional shelters and eight hundred latrines in their compounds. In all, we had helped make thousands of mud houses livable by repairing or completely rebuilding them.

These were lasting investments by the global community to help provide effective crisis response with long-term benefits. People had their dignity restored, and they regained their respect as they worked, served, and shared with others. We are thankful to donors like WFP, USAID, and OFDA for the food and funds they so generously provided. We also thank God for the wisdom and common sense he gave us to know how to use these resources in a most effective way.

This approach united the entire extended community of DQ. The thirteen villages that participated in our Host Family Project rallied around our desire to reduce the population of the open-air IDP camp. The project required significant local contributions and involvement; for every shelter we built or roof we repaired, we needed five woven bamboo mats and fifteen wooden beams. The village elders pulled together to provide these materials. Soon we had a caravan of camels, donkeys, horses, tractors, and small trucks delivering shelter supplies to our Nowabad office. Our two-basketball-court-sized yard overflowed with timber to be used for construction.

HEATING UP FOR WINTER

Winter's chilly arrival emphasized all the more the crucial need for hard shelter. The community worked feverishly to address this serious need. Once they realized they could directly impact their own future and help their neighbors, they molded themselves into an effective task force. The entire village resembled an anthill in high gear preparing for the cold months ahead.

The obvious need for heat offered other opportunities for us to mobilize the community. We transported tons of tin sheets from Tajikistan in order to manufacture wood-burning stoves. We hired local tinsmiths to train both IDP and local men to construct their own heaters. Our compound became a workstation. Every day men came to precisely measure and carefully cut tin and frame piping. Then they folded the trimmed sheets and attached them to the pipe frames, creating small-but-effective radiant, wood-burning heaters. During the frigid winter of 2000, we installed over two thousand wood stoves in Afghan homes.

Afghans also have a traditional heater called a *sandalee*. It resembles a tall coffee table made out of two-by-fours and a plywood top. The Afghan people have been constructing and using these safe, cost-effective heaters for centuries. They place a glowing pot of coals under the *sandalee;* then they cover the entire contraption with a large blanket (an afghan), thus containing most of the heat. This arrangement looks like the play tents children create by throwing blankets over tables and chairs. On cold nights, members of a household sit around the *sandalee,* facing the heater. Each person slides his or her feet under the blanket, then pulls it around himself or herself. The heat circulates under the material, warming the entire family. We hired experienced local carpenters, and thus invested in the local economy, to make around two thousand *sandalees*.

LOSING FACE

I've learned many hard lessons while in Afghanistan. Some of them have even been humiliating. The following one is particularly unforgettable. Like most lasting lessons, this one began with a mistake . . . mine.

We were about to do another major wheat distribution for WFP. This time we had over four thousand families on our registration lists. The plan called for us to give two fifty-kilogram bags of wheat to each IDP family. This may sound like a huge project, but we had been doing distributions this size for some time and had a system in place. I thought I was becoming quite good at them and was probably a little overconfident about our continued success.

As it often is in Afghanistan, the main question was, "Would the thirty-five 18-wheel trucks make it to Nowabad?" Logistical issues are one of the main difficulties in carrying out relief work. I had to constantly remind myself that this is Central Asia, which means things can and will change. It is not a matter of *if* but *when*. So, flexibility is the name of the game.

WFP sent us the beneficiary cards/coupons and we prepared some for distribution. Our goal was to start the distribution with the families who lived the farthest from us, because they would be the closest to the front line. We decided to give them priority. This was also helpful because it allowed us to divide the distribution in half. We doubted that all thirty-five trucks would arrive at the same time anyway. Gas shortages, snow, and muddy roads always brought a fresh conspiracy to thwart our carefully made plans.

We targeted the little villages closest to Dasht-e Qaleh itself. All these families were within range of the Taliban shelling. We would serve them first, because the front line could break any moment. This was a typical strategy for distribution, and our staff and the local authorities accepted our approach.

We prepared the coupons and distributed them to each family at the local mosque. Since I participated in our original surveys of this area and had frequent previous contacts with these families, I considered the procedure enjoyable and relatively easy. Many of these families had become my friends. When we got word via radio that the wheat was nearing, we selected a distribution site and informed the families from the designated villages. Because of muddy roads, possible Taliban jets, and the magnitude of this distribution, we actually had selected three alternate sites for daily distributions.

I love this part of our work. I've made it a point to be at almost every distribution, especially for food. By now, I even felt somewhat prepared and experienced. Uncharacteristically, this distribution went off almost without a hitch. Roughly half the trucks arrived, the people gathered, and we handed out the wheat.

After finishing the first round of distributions that involved about two thousand families, we got ready for the next round. We started with the same procedure as usual, preparing the coupons. I divided our staff of twelve into four teams to write the remaining two thousand coupons.

Handling the surveys, selecting beneficiaries, writing coupons, and distributing food involved a lot of work. I had to admit later that dropping food from an airplane is faster and easier. But the downside is that donors of the food never know who receives their assistance. Those who need help the most may not be able to get to the drop site, and if they do, they may simply be pushed aside by those who are bigger and stronger. We invested hours, days, and sometimes weeks in this life-saving work because we wanted to be sure that little orphan boys like Amonulah (a boy featured in an ABC television interview with me) got the food they needed. In order for "the least of these" to receive, someone on the ground had to supervise.

That's where groups like Shelter for Life become important. We put a face and a life with a gift. Our presence denies false reports, like the ones circulated in some Arab newspapers that the U.S. was lacing their air-dropped food with poison. We do our best to see to it that help gets to the people who need it most. We're here for all the people. We serve even the poorest of the poor. However, our work is not perfect, and I have learned so much from the experiences . . . and the mistakes.

I gathered my teams to process the remaining two thousand coupons. Those coupons would allow over ten thousand people to receive some hot bread. I unlocked my little tin safe to divvy out the two thousand cards to my staff but, to my shock, found the box empty. I couldn't find the cards. They were gone. My first thought was, *Some crooked Afghan stole our wheat cards.* I'm glad I didn't open my mouth and say that.

When I told our staff about the missing cards, they responded with shame, disappointment, and fear. They were sure that someone had stolen them.

"Who would do such a thing?" they kept asking one another.

I threw in my two cents' worth. "One of us had to have done it, and it wasn't me. I don't need the wheat or the coupons. I have money to buy my own bread."

Looking back, those words seem even more arrogant and prideful than they probably sounded that day. I even made other foolish comments: "Someone took them. They didn't just fly away."

We sat in a state of shock, overwhelmed by the tragedy. We had just lost over two hundred thousand pounds of wheat.

I informed our other two offices about the unfortunate situation.

Our staff in Rostaq said, "Mr. John, you took all the coupons to Nowabad, and since you guys already gave out half, they must have been lost, misplaced, or stolen in Nowabad."

My staff remained horrified. I hadn't actually accused any individuals, but they all felt as if I might point the finger at one of them or one of their relatives at any moment. Some were thinking, *I did tell others about the coupons and the upcoming wheat delivery.* They wondered if they had given out information that someone had used to carry out the theft. Each of them was afraid that somehow they would be implicated in this terrible act.

Shame spread throughout the community as the word of "Mr. John's missing WFP coupons" became the hot topic. In this part of the world and within Islamic society, you could be killed for such actions. I could almost hear the thief's accusers shouting, "You shamed our guest, the man who has been serving us, the American on the front line risking his life. You stole, and now we will all be cursed." They would have stoned, hanged, or beaten that thief to death for all to see. They would have probably also performed special rituals to rid the land and their lives of the curse this evil might bring upon them.

Uncertain about what to do next, I drove up the mountain to our Rostaq office to monitor our work there. I really needed to get away because this was eating at me. When I arrived at the office, the staff was preparing 110 coupons for our WFP wheat distribution in nearby Chah Ab. Another dagger pierced my heart when I saw those cards. I reviewed my days in Rostaq before taking the cards to Nowabad. I talked it through with the guys and retraced my steps to no avail.

What should I do? Should I report the theft to my good friend, the governor of Dasht-e Qaleh, and/or to the main commander? I hesitated to do that, because in an attempt to save my reputation (which would save their own, since they are in charge), they might take drastic actions to find the culprit. They would probably send soldiers to check every IDP family. I could not imagine five thousand families, who had been forced by the Taliban to leave their villages, now facing gun-toting soldiers whose instructions were to search them for the missing coupons.

I did report to the WFP in Feyzabad, because the cards and the wheat came from their office. Something had to be done. The remaining seventeen trucks were on the way and would arrive shortly. They understood and said they would reprint some cards and take them to our office in Feyzabad for us to deliver the next day to our office in Nowabad. I felt a little bit better. Perhaps this would all turn out fine.

Relieved, I pulled open one of my desk drawers for a worship tape to soothe my nerves. There in plain sight sat the packet of missing cards. I stared at them in disbelief. I wanted so much to just close the drawer, whistle, and say to myself, "John, don't ever tell anyone your foolish mistake. WFP is sending more cards; you can just get rid of this packet, and no one will ever know." But Someone would know. God knows and sees everything. Did I really want to be robbed of his peace? Even more to the point, I knew that my staff was under a huge cloud of fear, guilt, suspicion, and shame. I dared not keep this from them. This truth would set them . . . and me, free. If I hid the truth, I would be guilty of a conscious sin, rather than just an honest mistake.

First, I did what any good Central Asian would do: I talked with the old gray-bearded guys who worked for me. Gray hair and age are highly respected in Islamic and Asian cultures. I wanted their support, their wisdom, and their involvement. I also wanted their forgiveness.

Of course, they were relieved. However, they were deeply disappointed with me.

They quietly asked, "John, how could you do this? How could you be so irresponsible? You are not only the ex-pat in charge, but you're an expert in the eyes of others. Everyone admires you, respects you, and thinks you are next to God. Why John, why?"

The shame they had all been feeling came flying back to land like a huge weight on my shoulders. I instantly apologized with tears. I had no excuse, particularly for my readiness to accuse others for what I had done.

At first they didn't want me to tell anyone else. They were afraid that I would "lose face," which is a huge issue in Afghanistan and many Eastern countries. Since I was put in such a high position as a foreigner, an American, an aid worker in charge of a major project, they were concerned that others would lose respect for me if they knew of my carelessness and foolishness. They were concerned for my reputation and theirs as well. They might lose face, too, because they worked for me. They were afraid others would say, "Did you hear what Mr. John did? He lost the coupons and then accused his staff of being a bunch of dishonest thieves."

Well, we talked it through, and I was able to persuade them that I needed to publicly own up to my mistake. I planned to apologize to our whole staff, since my mistake reflected poorly on all of them. I was convinced that I must tell them the truth so they would be free from their own shame and fear. So I immediately called in all ten members of the staff, including the cook. I even wanted to include our watchdog Gurk, which means "wolf," but I knew that might be taking it a little too far.

I actually *wanted* everyone to know. I knew how liberating it would be for all of us. Everyone should know what had come from my carelessness. So I confessed to our staff and said I was sorry for this mistake. I apologized for thinking one of them might have stolen the cards. I asked them to forgive me for causing great fear and suspicion among us.

I sensed both their relief and their disappointment. I realized they were let down that I, their leader, made such a grave error. Over and over I apologized and reassured them that we were a team working together. I went through the painful process of going around the circle, eyeball-to-eyeball, with each staff person, saying, "Engineer Atiq, I am sorry. Will you please forgive me?" I actually wanted them to hear me say this, and I wanted to hear them say, "Yes, I forgive you." In this culture it is common to hold grudges and seek revenge, which is one of the reasons behind a lot of the tribal fighting. I wanted this unfortunate case closed, with no grudges left to hold.

My journal entry reads, "November 9, 2000, an utterly humiliating Thursday." But it was also freeing, healing, and relieving for all of us. Confession *is* good for the soul. I was so thankful that the cloud of doubt, rumor, suspicion, fear, and shame had blown away. The truth did set us all free. We were free to forgive, free to clear our consciences, and free to get on with life. I felt like shouting with Martin Luther King Jr.: "Free at last; free at last. Thank God Almighty, I'm free at last!"

Thankfully, my friends were able to show mercy to me in this situation, which is uncommon in the Central Asian culture. God's grace came to me through them. My mistake allowed them to experience what it's like to be a channel of God's kindness as I received forgiveness from them and God.

In Afghan society, people don't easily forget the past; it is usually bottled up until an opportune time to turn it into revenge. Gratefully, my act of carelessness actually turned into a wonderful experience and an opportunity to humbly emphasize for my Afghan friends that we are all sinners in need of a Savior.

Bone Weary, Burned Out, but Blessed

DASHT-E QALEH—My first four months in Afghanistan flew by in a blur of nonstop activity. Near the end of 2000, if someone had asked me at the time how I was feeling, I would have said, "Hey, I'm too busy to burn out." Still, there were moments when I felt completely overwhelmed by the enormity of what needed to be done.

The work fulfilled my longing to be useful, but it was always with me. I have since realized that people don't burn out doing something they don't like; they more likely burn out doing what they're passionate to accomplish. Our passion consumes us. I was finally putting my passion into action, but the need was far greater than my best efforts could meet. I found myself bone weary in every possible way.

My journal entries during these weeks catalog a growing impatience and exhaustion. On November 17, I noted the following events of the day:

> Ate some bread, tea, and milk. Balanced our accounts and paid all our weekly bills. Since it was raining and Juma [Friday], our supposed day off, I decided to stay home. Really getting frustrated with all the delays of

this distribution. A four-day job may take four weeks. But there is grace. Thankfully, we put a wood stove in our room and bathroom today. Waiting for the trucks of wheat to come, so found some more quiet time. Lord, my heart is longing to do some development work, because this relief work is draining and demanding. May your mercy, O God, sustain me!

Certain built-in frustrations come with the work. As much as I enjoy learning foreign languages, I certainly don't mind speaking English. Those early months in Afghanistan gave me very few opportunities for face-to-face, easy conversations. Even the simplest discussion with the national staff required a lot of energy and concentration on my part.

SPEAK OR SERVE

I also understood and fully accepted the limitations imposed on me as a Christian relief worker in a Muslim country. However, the day-to-day lack of interaction about my faith was exasperating. I had come to teach, to start an educational institute, to be a communicator, but instead I was overwhelmed by the tyranny of the urgent needs around me. I found it hard to keep my mouth shut when what I wanted to do was run down the streets shouting about the goodness and grace of God.

I knew that my efforts in Afghanistan had real value, for our presence and programs were saving lives. But, in reality, I felt the situation was almost completely out of control. Because of my frantic schedule, I rarely had time to speak about my beliefs. Actually, I became a service-oriented workaholic and it showed. In fact, it was wearing me out.

Afghans seemed to ask about my faith in moments when I felt least worthy to talk about it. And sometimes I was so tired that I lacked the sensitivity to see that some were sincerely seeking. Then when I was primed and ready to tell the world the good news of the gospel, no one asked. Many times I felt I wasn't doing all I could to communicate the love of God.

SPIRITUAL ENCOUNTERS

Although I remember these months as a dry and difficult time, my journal notes remind me that there were always unusual interactions. Ramadan, or Ramazan, the month when all Muslims fast from sunrise to sunset, included numerous spiritual encounters. In 2000, Ramazan began on November 27. I observed the fast along with our national staff, which raised both eyebrows and questions. Since that Muslim season promotes spiritual seeking and religious rituals, many people expressed curiosity about my faith.

One night in Nowabad, I was invited to dinner with our neighbors. They wanted to express their gratitude for my efforts with a gift of hospitality. Reciprocity lies behind many social interactions in the Asian world. My side of the balance far outweighed theirs, in the eyes of many people in Dasht-e Qaleh. They assumed I personally provided most of what we distributed. I could not explain to them that, in terms of material possessions, many of them owned more than I did. They felt compelled to serve me out of a sense of debt. I didn't want to be an added burden in their struggle to survive, but I realized their gesture had more to do with their dignity than my comfort.

I went to dinner that night with my good friend Engineer Massoud and one of our project managers, whom I called Ali Khan. He's a likable, jolly, old fellow who knows some English. That evening, when it was appropriate to break the daily fast, we walked to Saed Akbar's house. Twelve of us had been invited for the occasion. Most of the guests were village elders, either from the IDP community or the local population of Nowabad.

First we dedicated the feast by intoning the customary *Bismillah,* Arabic for "in the name of God." Then we began to eat the delicious assortment of foods placed on the cloth that was spread on the carpeted floor. Among the delicacies were several versions of the famous Afghan pilaf—a rice dish that contains diced carrots and raisins. Lamb and beef kabobs, sizzling their mouth-watering aromas, rested atop the edible mounds. Bread and hot tea accompanied the meal. After the main course we had fruit, almonds, and pistachios. Eating in Afghanistan requires reaching across the table. This was a typical meal of genuine Central Asian kindness and gracious hospitality.

Finally someone asked, as if on cue, "Mr. John, why are you fasting?"

I briefly explained how followers of Jesus Christ also practice fasting as a spiritual discipline. That led to a number of comments around the dinner cloth about the purposes of fasting.

As the interest in that subject waned, another man asked, "Mr. John, who is Jesus Christ?"

My mouth dropped, but I was able to respond in a mixture of broken Uzbek and Dari, deeply honored by their curiosity. Stumped at times, I even used some English, which Ali Khan graciously translated. My brief audience was attentive and respectful. When I finished, they nodded thoughtfully, and the discussion moved on to other matters.

Afterwards, Ali remarked, "Mr. John, you told them the whole story!"

I wondered how that evening affected those men.

Just prior to Christmas, John Caleb, my teammate, joined two of our key local staff and me for a meeting with the main commander of Rostaq. The commander's deputy and the mayor also attended. Normally, such a gathering required the host to serve hot tea and sweets to his guests. We declined, along with our Muslim fellow guests, because we were all still keeping Ramazan. The commander was obviously surprised but also quite pleased. Foreigners seldom know about or observe their local customs.

He, also being a respected religious elder, began quoting from the Koran about Ramazan. Then he added a number of comments about Jesus Christ that he had read in his Muslim holy book. Now it was my turn to be surprised and pleased.

He turned to me and asked, "Mr. John, do you believe Jesus Christ is alive?"

I looked down to see where I dropped my heart. I replied, *"Albata,"* which means "of course" in both Uzbek and Dari.

The commander looked at me calmly, expecting me to continue. He wanted the long version. Again I fumbled with language, bouncing back and forth from Uzbek and Dari. Because of the season, I briefly described the significance of Christmas. Having read his holy book I used the areas of common ground to build a bridge for communication. But I tried to make crystal clear the "reason for the season."

As I struggled to communicate without offending, I noticed that our two local staff men and the mayor were not interested in our religious dialogue. One of our Afghan staff member's faces took on an embarrassed shade of crimson. It was as if he was afraid someone would think he shared the same feelings about the Messiah as Mr. John.

I have found that fear is the main obstacle that keeps Easterners and Asians from seriously considering the teachings of Christ. It still amazes me that millions of people are held captive to various religious systems simply out of fear. I also fear God, but I wonder at times if it is the same flavor of fear. Our conversation about spiritual matters that day ended as someone politely reminded us that we had work to do.

CHRISTMAS

By the time Christmas 2000 rolled around, I had been working every day for four months, and knew I needed rest. I had arrived in the country with one bag and a one-week itinerary. This was the first opportunity I'd had to take a breather and travel back to our central field office in Dushanbe, Tajikistan. We were also scheduled to spend time with our staff and leadership in Dushanbe, since we with Shelter for Life needed to consider ways to expand and better serve the Afghan people. I looked forward to the change of pace and scenery.

Caleb and I arranged our plans to travel from Rostaq to Tajikistan via Feyzabad for Christmas. But winter tossed a thick blanket on our plans. At first, the possibility of spending the holidays snowbound in Afghanistan frustrated me. I felt a little homesick. The heavy snows meant that I had a whiter Christmas in Central Asia than most people back in Coats, North Carolina, or many other places in my own country. We even thought the weather might keep us from the annual meetings in Tajikistan in early January.

Since we had a television, VCR, and a generator at the Shelter for Life office, we decided to watch some movies. Like the old Christmas song with a twist, "The weather outside is frightful, but our wood-stove fire is so delightful, and since to Dushanbe we cannot go, let it snow, let it snow, let it snow." We seized the opportunity and watched the film *Jesus,* which portrays the life of Christ from the Gospel according to Saint Luke. The English soundtrack gave me the longest dose of my own language that I had heard in months.

Two other events made our Christmas holidays even more special. During the autumn, our Rostaq office sponsored some beginning English classes, taught by one of our local staff in a little classroom we had built. They met every day, and Christmas was no exception. The instructor invited us to visit as his guest English teachers. As a result, we had the privilege of telling the story of Jesus the Messiah.

The following day we set out for Feyzabad in hopes of catching a flight to Dushanbe. Thanks to our skillful and determined driver, we arrived safely through the snow some six hours later. Soon we would be gathering again. This time we viewed the *Jesus* film in Dari. It was my language lesson for the day. Four Afghan friends joined three of us Americans for the evening. I realized during those hours that I was celebrating Christmas at its finest. No tree, no presents, no lights—simply companionship and conversation about Jesus the Messiah.

WINTER WONDERLAND

ESHKASHEM—At this time, there were only three ways to leave northeast Afghanistan. The UN maintained an occasional flight in and out of Feyzabad. And two border crossings still offered access to Tajikistan, if they were open. Our obvious choice for travel was the Ay Khanom border, just a few miles from my house in Dasht-e Qaleh. But it was closed because the Taliban bombed it every day in hopes of cutting off General Massoud's pipeline of military resources. The other border was in a remote area south and east of Feyzabad at Eshkashem.

Two of my friends from Shelter for Life, Seth and Caleb, and I waited in Feyzabad for a UN plane. But the weather prevented any flights to or from the country. Once we realized we could be stuck for the rest of the holidays, I began to relax. Feyzabad became an oasis in the desert of exhaustion. I didn't have many responsibilities there, so I could rest, practice the language, and visit with friends.

A week after Christmas, the UN made it official: The next flight to Dushanbe would be "whenever weather permitted." By then no planes had flown for two weeks. If the weather continued to leave us grounded, we would miss the annual planning meetings and most of the R&R we had planned in Tajikistan. So we called our regional director in Dushanbe to chat about our dilemma. He encouraged us to try for the "unknown border" at Eshkashem. No one from our agency had ever been within miles of it.

The road from Feyzabad to the Eshkashem border passes through scenic and unforgettable terrain. We headed toward the great Vakhan Valley that forms the panhandle of northeast Afghanistan, which stretches through towering peaks to touch the western frontier lands of China. The road wound between snow-capped mountains and breathtaking drop-offs. We retraced the steps of countless caravans and armies that had followed the Silk Road for millennia. In spite of the frigid temperatures, we stopped occasionally to enjoy the beauty of God's creation.

Before we set out, we hired Bobojon, a driver from another nongovernment organization. He had just taken some of his international staff to this same border, and we wanted to take advantage of his familiarity with the terrain. Bobojon proved to be an added value when we arrived at the border at three o'clock in the afternoon, after they had already closed it. In other circumstances, we would have been stranded and chilly in our vehicle overnight. Instead, our driver became our tour guide.

He took us to the home of Baz Mohammed up in the snow-filled hills of Eshkashem. Baz became our host. Hospitality is the rule in Afghan culture. We ate *kabali pilov,* some bread, and drank a lot of hot tea. Baz assured us he felt honored to have three Afghan-looking Americans stay with him.

When he showed us to our room, we discovered that its most remarkable feature was the lack of panes in the windows. We had a roof over our heads, but the temperature inside the room was about the same as the temperature outside. For a bathroom we had the great outdoors, where frostbite awaited the daring. We fired up a small wood stove to take the chill off the room and huddled under the pile of blankets Baz provided. We thanked God for his protection and asked his blessing on the home of Baz Mohammed, who had given us a warm welcome on a frigid night.

In the morning, we carefully refilled the radiator we had drained the night before. It's just one of those added chores in a land with no supply of antifreeze. Baz added some boiling water to the radiator to help thaw the oil. Then we gathered for prayer around the green Russian Jeep, asking the Lord to bless us with enough battery power to start the engine. It cleared its throat several times, then ran with the familiar chug of the previous day.

Breakfast at the Baz Mohammed inn consisted mostly of drinking *shir-choy* (milk-tea, with a pinch of salt and sugar) from a soup bowl. The name sounds a little like "sheer joy," but the taste is something else. This is a traditional drink in some areas of Afghanistan. Our driver Bobojon has since told many people about our adventure in great detail. As he tells it, his most memorable moment was drinking *shir-choy* with three Afghan-looking Americans, who were trying the drink for the first time. We had stumbled onto an important cultural rite of passage. Some country-side Afghans like to say, "You're really one of us if you drink *shir-choy.*"

We finally arrived at the border late in the morning. We fortunately picked up the chief Afghan official on the way. Otherwise, we would have waited even longer. He walks three miles every day from town to the border, if he wants to work in the freezing cold. He unlocked the gate and wished us well.

TROUBLE IN TAJIKISTAN

TAJIKISTAN—The welcome we got on the Tajik side of no-man's-land was less than enthusiastic. They weren't expecting three scruffy Americans. One of them (me) greeted them in Russian, switched to broken Tajik (which they call really good Dari), and even occasionally threw in an Uzbek word when appropriate. When they asked for our papers, they were in for another surprise. One of us (me again) did not have an NGO (nongovernment organization) identification card, because I came for only a week and then stayed for four months. Another of the guys with me was carrying an expired identification card. We were so obviously suspicious that they were convinced we should probably be kept out of their country. Our initial explanations made no impression whatsoever on the guardians of the border.

We called the regional office in Dushanbe via Codan radio and asked for some advice. Our regional director told us that he had spoken with a Tajik general, who had given us verbal permission to enter Tajikistan. Since this culture operates on a chain of command system, we talked to the border guards as if we really knew General Jalil. Name dropping helped, but the gate remained closed.

All three of us were worn out from the cold, the wind, and the headache of arguing. We knew they had us just where they wanted us. Three infuriated Americans at the border, held up and helpless in the hands of Russian/Tajik soldiers. Their enjoyment over our predicament was obvious and for me was one of the hardest experiences of my life. Looking back, I realize that it revealed just how little energy and good attitude I had left to share. We were frustrated and felt that they were taking advantage of us. I'm definitely not proud of my attitude and actions that day.

When they finally were ready to let us cross, some five hours later, they decided to check everything that we had, and I mean everything.

One of the soldiers said rather sarcastically, "We have to do all of this at our KGB checkpoint *offices.*"

I looked at the shabby, windowless, heatless metal container they used for an office, angered by the senseless delays. I distinctly remember thinking in North Carolinian style, *Man, this is no office. You don't even have a pen that writes. You're using my pen (his had frozen) to write my name on a scrap piece of paper and look through my stuff, as if I'm some kind of prisoner.*

Then, instead of thinking before speaking, I muttered under my breath, "If I were reacting as a sinner, I would blow up your *office.*"

They checked through everything the three of us had. It took about an hour. Then they called the main Russian general. He showed up decked out in uniform with a stern, strong look and asked the same set of questions we had already answered at least three times. Speaking through a Tajik soldier as his translator (thankfully this guy understood my broken Dari), his final question was, "Sir, why did you say you would blow up our office?"

I was speechless at first. How did he know I said such a thing? I had mumbled those words in English. None of the soldiers had given any indication they understood my mother tongue. All I could do was apologize profusely. I assured him that I hadn't meant those words and that I had no means or authority to carry out such a foolish statement. He apparently understood my shame and accepted my regrets, because he shook my hand and said we could go across the border.

Once we passed through the border gate, another surprise awaited us. There is no town on the Tajik side. The closest village is four miles away, and we were now on foot. We hitched a ride into town from a man at the border, who also agreed to take us to Khorugh for a price. That was the closest city from which we thought we could get a flight on Tajik Air into Dushanbe. Instead of heading north, however, the driver went the opposite direction and straight to the local KGB office.

At the time, this was extremely frustrating because of everything we had already been through at the border. Later, it turned out to be a fortuitous event, because I ended up sleeping in the very same KGB office nine months later. We checked in with the KGB and explained once more why we had come into the country. I made sure not to make any comments under my breath about blowing things up. After the usual round of endless questions and surprises at what they considered to be my expert linguistic skills, we were on our way to Khorugh. By this time it was afternoon.

Before long we encountered more aggravations. Our route

included frequent checkpoints. It almost made my blood boil when we were stopped and searched at every one of them. When we finally arrived in Khorugh, we had no idea where to stay. We told the driver to take us to a hotel. We found only one, which I remember as the "drunk" hotel. The lobby chairs and couches held nothing but badly inebriated people. The lady and man who appeared to run the place didn't even have enough strength to greet us. So we decided to try elsewhere.

Our driver then remembered that an NGO in town had a guest house. We eventually found the office of FOCUS, a relief and development NGO that is connected with the Agha Khan Foundation. They were surprised to see three bearded Americans at such an hour, but they graciously agreed to house us for the night.

Before our driver left, he inquired about our hunger. He offered to feed us. In all the commotion, we hadn't eaten anything since our *shir-choy* for breakfast. He took us to the house of some relatives for a candlelight experience, since the electricity had gone out in town. This is a common occurrence in many areas of the former Soviet Union. We sat in a ten-story, Communist-era, block apartment and nearly froze to death while the cook struggled to prepare food for us in a dark and powerless kitchen.

Finally, amidst warm Tajik hospitality, dinner was served. It was delicious, though I can't report what we ate. I couldn't identify the components of the meal in the dimness of the candlelight. Afterward, our driver took us back to the guest house, where we got some much-needed rest. We all slept in one room, taking advantage of the meager heat the three of us produced.

Our morning in Khorugh began with an unexpected hearty breakfast of eggs, toast, fruit, cheese, and Russian sausage. After thanking our hosts, we packed and proceeded by foot to the bazaar. Our plan was to rent some local transport that would take us all the way to Dushanbe. The snow had again ruled out any chances of a Tajik Air flight. We would have to take the long way home. At the car area of the market I negotiated a ride for one hundred dollars in an old green military-looking Russian Jeep. Little did we know that we were in for the ride of our lives.

ANGEL IN DISGUISE

DUSHANBE—Our journey to Dushanbe turned into a twenty-seven-hour, nonstop marathon. The way was again replete with checkpoints. This time Caleb, along with our new friend Rahim, did the negotiating honors. We picked up Rahim, who was going to Dushanbe for a company meeting. In Central Asia, there is always room for one more when traveling. I gave up all communication duties and sat in the very back of the Jeep, sandwiched between seats and luggage.

Rahim turned out to be an angel in disguise. At a few checkpoints, the guns and the smell of vodka made us wonder about the intent of those manning the post. Rahim became our wise spokesman; he could speak as a genuine cultural insider. Thankfully, we didn't get shot or robbed. A few times we gave some candy or food to guards, or the driver shared his cigarettes. Our gifts and gestures of peace probably saved our lives and possessions on more than one occasion.

Our story could be as long and tiresome as the trip. At times we barely made it through the snow. The mountain driving in Tajikistan shares many hair-raising similarities with the driving in Afghanistan. Some of our only pit stops were when the car broke down, and we still don't know how our driver managed to make repairs in the dark. But we finally reached Dushanbe at eleven o'clock the next morning and stumbled into the apartment I had supposedly left for just a few days four months earlier. How refreshing it was to take a hot shower and then lay down for some uninterrupted rest.

Seeing friends and coworkers in Tajikistan refreshed me emotionally too. Our annual meetings were enjoyable. We were able to pray, reminisce, plan, strategize, and look to the future with a sense of hope.

During our discussions, our regional director informed us that our vision for our role in Afghanistan was expanding. We made some plans to start an educational institute, a community health program, and various reconstruction projects that would help the Afghans rebuild their infrastructure. The results of this extremely long and exhausting trip turned out to be exactly what I needed. I returned to Feyzabad in early February 2001 refreshed and eager to resume my duties inside Afghanistan.

SCHOOL DAYS, SCHOOL DAYS

NOWABAD—The success of our Host Family Project kept me busy during much of the early part of the year and well into the summer. Gradually, as people settled into substantial housing, my concerns turned elsewhere. We still had a full schedule of distributions, but I wanted to give more attention to development projects.

One day in April of 2001, I received a visit from two men who were a part of the IDP commission in the Rostaq area. In each area, several men were designated as the *shura* leaders or elders for the displaced community. These two men were teachers from Khvajeh Ghar. They wanted me to help them start an educational program for the boys and girls of the refugee population. They had my enthusiastic support almost instantly, of course.

As a teacher, I believe strongly in education. I also enjoy how much I always learn while I'm teaching. But how do we provide education for wandering, displaced refugees? I had no experience with this problem. I told the two men that, if they were willing to organize the school, I would help provide the funds, the rent, the place, the materials, and the support. I told them to survey the IDP families, register the students (girls and boys), and develop a list of those willing and qualified to teach, both men and women.

These men returned in only a few days with startling results. They had a list of over eight hundred elementary-aged students, about half girls, half boys. They had also identified twenty-eight teachers, including twelve women, who could staff the school. I was ecstatic!

I looked up from their lists and said, "We have to find a place."

One of them handed me another list. "Here are some places we think might be available for such a school."

I couldn't help but smile. These two men were way ahead of me. One of the places on their list turned out to be ideal. We negotiated an arrangement with the owner for just one hundred dollars rent for the entire school year, with the added stipulations that we would dig a well and build two latrines. The temporary wooden-bamboo, hut-type classrooms we planned to build would remain with the property. He was pleased, and we were in the education business.

I hired Akbar, our carpenter friend, and told him to train IDPs to help him build four large, wooden-bamboo structures that would protect the students and teachers from the sun but would allow plenty of air for coolness. Later we divided these into eight classrooms.

The property already had four rooms (one would be a teachers' office). We got a mason busy on the well and some of our construction supervisors to build the latrines. We hired some local men to make chalkboards. I called some other agencies to provide textbooks, and within a week we had all the components for a full-blown school under construction or slated for delivery. The first day of class in May 2001 brought out more than eight hundred fifty students. We then started a school in Desht-e Qaleh for another eight hundred displaced children.

It was exciting to see both boys and girls learning. Their presence represented much-needed hope for the future. It was also a way of restoring dignity to the teachers. They were now working, using their skills to help serve their own people. The women, in particular, were so grateful that we provided work for them and education for their children, including their daughters. The full impact of what we were doing in Afghanistan didn't really hit me until months later.

WORK FOR WHEAT

ROSTAQ—The road from Rostaq to Dasht-e Qaleh gave me my original crash course in Afghan travel. I never forgot the experience. I traveled that road so frequently I could instinctively brace myself for its every bump. I gradually made it my mission to find a way to improve the popcorn-popping ride it offered.

The Host Family Project had often demonstrated the value of labor. In spite of the massive amounts of free aid that we distributed during my early months in Dasht-e Qaleh, I found people eager to work. When we proposed the Host Family Project, we gave homeowners the incentive of improvements to their houses in exchange for their willingness to host IDPs. But we also insisted that both the homeowners and the IDPs help with building the extra rooms, latrines, and doing repairs. To ensure this, we offered wheat in lieu of cash payments for their labor. The enthusiastic response told us we had hit on an effective principle. Other subprojects, like the manufacturing of tin wood stoves and *sandalees,* further demonstrated the principle of dignity through work. We hired skilled men, who instructed both homeowners and IDPs in the production of these items. In the process, some of these learners discovered they had skills that could translate into provision for their families.

People in places like Afghanistan know that there are many things better than money. If a wealthy man is starving, but there is no food to buy, his money doesn't taste very good. In providing hard goods or food in exchange for labor, we applied a principle of bartering that predates money. Sometimes it's the only workable choice.

One of the bone-jarring ruts on the Rostaq-to-Dasht-e Qaleh

road finally got my attention. I suddenly realized I was driving on top of a big enough project to occupy thousands of men for months. I decided right then and there to propose the use of our work-for-wheat arrangement for a large-scale project. Fifty kilometers of handmade road didn't equate to the Pyramids, but it was certainly a worthy challenge.

Actually, the Rostaq-to-Dasht-e Qaleh road probably already carried traffic when the Egyptians were busy building their amazing monuments. Countless hooves of camels, horses, and herds wore out paths that wooden wheels and rubber tires had then followed through the centuries. Unfortunately, the hard-packed clay that easily supports animal traffic becomes a slick, impassable surface for cars and trucks when wet. Where one horse easily passes, a multi-horsepower vehicle sits helpless, wheels spinning furiously.

We made a careful study of that stretch of road. The roadbed could support heavy vehicles, but we needed to add gravel to the surface to increase traction in all kinds of weather. The road also needed widening in places. Wherever we noted outcroppings of stone along the road, we marked them. We also identified stretches with inclines or clay surfaces that needed extra traction treatment. Then we at Shelter for Life approached Tearfund-UK with the concept and our need for cash to implement it. They gladly and eagerly agreed to supply the funds. And the USAID wheat we needed for payment to the laborers would come from our contractual agreement with World Food Programme.

Work on the road began in earnest during the spring of 2001. We busied crews digging out the large rocks and breaking them up with mauls. No steam shovels or earth-moving equipment were used here—just good, old-fashioned manpower. Loads of hand-crushed stone was transported on heavy-duty stretchers by pairs of workers or donkeys and dumped at the designated locations. Slowly the improvements began to take shape. And it continues even today.

This project was designed to employ at least eight thousand workers. Payment in wheat will eventually benefit almost fifty thousand family members with food. The work has restored dignity and self-respect to these men, who have been able to work with their hands to provide for their families. They have gained a sense of belonging, self-worth, and pride as they have helped improve the quality of life for their families and thousands of others.

A Touch of Freedom

UNITED STATES—By the time July arrived, I was ready for another break outside the country. Our work was shifting steadily toward a greater emphasis on long-term development, even though the situation in the war with the Taliban showed no signs of changing. It even appeared that I might be able to invest a significant amount of my time in educational projects that showed promise. But I needed a short rest, and I knew I could only get that outside the country.

At the advice of Shelter for Life, I flew all the way back to the U.S., arriving home in time for the Fourth of July. My visit quickly turned into a working holiday, with meetings at the OFDA and USAID offices in Washington D.C. The buildings in and around D.C. were overwhelming compared to my mud house in Dasht-e Qaleh. My homeland seemed invincible and untouchable.

The meetings in Washington went well. It was nice to be able to report to our main donor (the U.S. government) about our activities and use of their funds. I enjoyed presenting our work and trying to educate and inspire those who controlled the purse strings. Officials who watched the slide shows and heard the stories of success promised their continued support.

During that time, I was staying with my grandmother, who lives in northern Virginia. I found myself continually amazed by the beauty and bounty of our country. Time spent with family and friends refreshed me. The festivities surrounding the Fourth of July repeatedly drove home for me the priceless heritage I have been given. I had just arrived from a war-torn nation that was struggling with the despair of a raging civil war, to enjoy all the benefits and responsibilities of genuine liberty. I was overwhelmed and humbled, joyous and grateful.

Within days I realized that one of the ways I most enjoy celebrating my freedom involves reaching out to help those less fortunate than I am, in the hope that they might find the same kind of freedom. While serving in Afghanistan, I had already learned the important lesson that America is not the only place that should be called "the home of the brave." Now I prepared for my return to Afghanistan with a renewed sense of purpose, believing that America is also not the only place that should be the "land of the free."

Friends under Fire

August 2001

AFGHANISTAN—After a short time outside the country, I eagerly headed back into Afghanistan in August. When I left for my break in July, we had recently set in motion several educational projects, and I could hardly wait to see their progress. But the raging war and border tensions conspired to make the journey difficult. The front lines between the Northern Alliance and the Taliban remained in the same place, but the two sides acted like evenly matched fighters who had just started a new round. They stood toe-to-toe in the center of the ring and exchanged blow after blow, neither gaining a decisive advantage.

Other developments intensified the situation in Afghanistan. A number of NGOs had been working in Kabul, assisting refugees in the Taliban-held territories. They functioned under extreme limitations imposed by the regime. The Taliban showed little interest or effort in helping their own people survive. But well-meaning westerners were allowed to provide humanitarian assistance, as long as the Taliban received credit for allowing the agencies to operate.

During the first week of August, the Taliban in Kabul suddenly exercised their erratic and treacherous understanding of the law. They arrested eight foreign workers from Shelter Now Germany that had historic ties with the U.S.-based SNI/Shelter for Life. I actually was on my way to Dulles International Airport for my return trip to Afghanistan when I heard about the arrest of the aid workers.

At first, I thought the detainees were from my own team. The news report mentioned "Shelter Now International in Afghanistan." I called Norm, our international director in Wisconsin, just before boarding my flight to Europe. I was anxious to know what had happened.

He said, "John, our friends in Kabul from SNI/Germany have been busted by the Taliban." He went on to tell me they had been accused of operating outside their permitted functions in a strict Muslim society. Among those imprisoned were two of our American friends—Heather Mercer and Dayna Curry.

We wondered if these developments would affect our work in the north. We also had to consider the fate of our activities in the West; in the ancient city of Herat we had begun a massive housing project under the noses of the Taliban. There we were again hoping to eliminate a humanitarian crisis by constructing four thousand shelters, including kitchens, bathhouses, and wells for the nearly quarter of a million displaced people who had migrated to the Maslakh Camp in that area.

Unfortunately, we soon had to evacuate our American project manager from Herat during the tense days of new restrictions by the Taliban. Thankfully, our dedicated local staff, at personal risk, continued the project during the imprisonment of the aid workers in Kabul and the invasion of the U.S.-led coalition forces. By God's favor, we still have a prominent presence and major programs in the western part of Afghanistan as one of the lead international organizations serving the war-torn, drought-stricken people in that region.

The arrest of international relief workers focused media attention on Kabul. We were often asked about the similarities between the names for Shelter for Life and Shelter Now Germany. Frankly, we had to be careful. Even acknowledging the previous partnership between the two organizations could have put the prisoners at risk. In the Taliban way of thinking, *connection* easily means *collusion*.

I lived with the acute awareness that, if the Taliban knew another Christian American was actively working inside Afghanistan, the Christians being held captive might well become targets for torturing. Even though the jailed personnel had no direct affiliation with Shelter for Life, we had great concern for their safety as fellow relief workers. Our hearts also cried daily for the national workers under arrest. They appeared to be destined for harsh, Taliban-style "justice"—the death penalty in a public place.

Every day, I asked God to set them free. I know hundreds of thousands of people around the world joined in this prayer. I was so relieved when the news came a few months later that all eight foreigners and sixteen nationals had been safely released. Truly they survived as "prisoners of hope."

But in August of 2001, the outlook for the group in Kabul looked grim. Some of the charges leveled carried with them a maximum sentence, and the Taliban threatened to treat the westerners with the same punishment they had planned for the Afghan captives. As a result of these allegations and accusations, several other organizations in Taliban-controlled areas suffered as well. Though our SNI/Shelter for Life offices in the north and west were not affected, many agencies had to close up shop as the tightened fists of the Taliban knocked them out of the country.

At the time, I still believed the best place for me was in Afghanistan. Thankfully, I could continue to supervise our projects in the north with the blessing of President Rabbani and General Massoud. Another staff person serving in a different area also intended to return. In mid-August we journeyed south together to join in the work that was already in motion.

Even with our area director's permission, the way into Northern Alliance territories presented a very real challenge. Flights in and out of Feyzabad seldom kept a schedule, and priority assignments for the limited seats dimmed our chances of getting on board. Then the Taliban threatened to shoot down UN airplanes, under the pretext that they were being used to transport military assistance for the Northern Alliance. Strict air security in Tajikistan, as well as Pakistan and Afghanistan, grounded all nonmilitary flights. If we really wanted to get back in the country, we would have to make arrangements on our own. That meant another long, arduous road trip.

Overland travel from Dushanbe to the Tajik border was measured not in kilometers or miles but in checkpoints. The Tajik military and the KGB maintained similar security sites, but each one seemed unique. We were usually questioned, our papers were checked, and our vehicle was searched before we could continue to the next one.

Sometimes we drove up to find the guardhouse deserted, and we would have to open the gate ourselves. Several times the metal boxcarlike containers were manned, but the guards inside were drunk. Lack of traffic and too much time and vodka on their hands made life miserable for these Tajik soldiers.

Between the checkpoints, the heavily rutted dirt roads or surfaces of cracked and broken pavement were in such poor condition that we bounced around like rubber balls. We tried to look on the bright side and make the best of the physical bruising we received on these trips, so we called them "Central Asian massages."

THE CROSSING

AMU DARYA RIVER—The border we wanted to use was officially closed because of the fighting. This entry point is actually on the Amu Darya River that separates Tajikistan from Afghanistan. The surrounding mountains that gradually fall into the river make this a scenic place. However, our awareness of the beauty had vanished by the time we arrived at the border itself.

It was the middle of the night, the preferred time for crossing the river. Fording in the dark was supposed to be less dangerous than during the day, when the Taliban could see at whom they were shooting. The Taliban regularly bombed the border, in order to cut off General Massoud's supply line from Tajikistan. That same bombing also cut off or drastically hindered NGOs from bringing assistance into northeast Afghanistan.

We stopped near the border to inform the Russian and Tajik guards of our desire to cross the river. They reminded us that the border was closed. We didn't bother asking why; by then we were close enough to hear the bombardment.

We persisted, and they countered that it didn't matter to them if we left. They just wanted to warn us that we *wouldn't* get across the river or into Afghanistan. After some friendly negotiations, we were able to talk them into lifting the gate to let us attempt a crossing. Several of the soldiers escorted us to the river. As we walked, they continually predicted that no one would be at the other side because of the bombings. But we pressed on, believing God would make a way.

That night taught me the meaning of the phrase "pitch dark." The only light came from the flashes of bombs landing nearby. These sometimes came so close that we all jumped into a nearby bunker.

One soldier kept mumbling, "This is not a good idea." His tone spoke his fear more clearly than his Tajik words.

When we arrived at the river, we discovered our escort was right—no one was visible on the Afghan side. We were stuck there. This border had no good way to contact the other side either. Signal lights were strongly discouraged for fear of enemy spotters.

Our friends fired a rifle into the air as a signal, but this provoked no response from the other shore. They didn't repeat the signal, because Afghans don't have ammunition to waste on Tajiks. Our Dushanbe driver and the border guards were petrified. After the gunshot, we waited, but no boat, raft, or barge materialized out of the darkness. Still convinced God would come through, my teammate and I quietly prayed.

The guards anxiously urged us to leave. Then I remembered that back in our vehicle we had a Codan radio we could use to call our Nowabad office on the other side of the river. This call had to be short and somewhat vague, because the Taliban often monitored our transmissions. We didn't want to give them any added incentives as they bombed the border that night. When I contacted Nowabad, they told us they had already sent a Jeep to meet us. So I switched frequencies and called our Jeep on the other side of the river to give the driver instructions.

I said, vaguely, in my American-accented Dari, "Please go tell the one in charge that Mr. John and a guest are at the other side."

Moments later we noticed movement on the far shore. The dull glow of hooded lights signaled their activity. Our Uzbek friends were coming.

The Amu Darya is over fifty yards across at this point, and the current moves swiftly. It's deep enough that it has swallowed tractor-trailers and a Russian vehicle barge that sank several years ago under fire. A curious assortment of smaller craft has since been used to transport military supplies into Afghanistan.

Crossings are often exciting and always dangerous. Fixed cables to assist in getting across the water simply present too tempting a target for the Taliban. Instead, a raft has to be dragged along the shore and launched a hundred yards or so upriver from the landing spot on the other side. That way, the river current helps those who are paddling to reach our shore at approximately the right place. Even so, it's much easier said than done. Doing this by daylight would have been challenging enough, but we added the complicating element of absolute darkness.

When our ride splashed onto the shore, we realized they had underestimated who and what needed transportation from our side of the river. They sent a young Uzbek soldier in a rubber raft about the size of a bathtub. He and the two of us would barely fit in it. Our chances of getting extremely wet soared in my mind. Unfortunately, we also had a lot of equipment with us—laptops, office supplies, and equipment—stuff that would not handle a river dunking well. Our raft had no room for our luggage either. I realized our courageous companion would have to make two crossings. So I got ready to give him my Uzbek version of a pep talk.

For a moment, I was in a frenzy about the arrangements, because I was sure that, as soon as we pushed off, our staff and the soldiers would get away from the river quickly because the bombing was still going on. I didn't blame them. Besides, could we ask this young rafter to risk his life again for a few computers, printers, a copy machine, and office supplies?

We got into the tiny raft to, in my British teammate's under-stated expression, "Give it a go." I asked our Tajik car driver to please wait, because we hoped the Uzbek soldier would indeed paddle back to get our stuff. If the raft did not return, he would have to carry the boxes back to the car and take them to Dushanbe. Everyone did his part in those tense minutes.

To my amazement, we crossed safely. Then our rendezvous rescuer bravely went back for our baggage and brought it all to us completely dry. He laughed as I shook his hand and thanked him profusely. Then I realized that this was all in a night's work for him.

On the Afghan side, we were greeted like a convoy of kings. The backslapping soldiers hugged us like heroes and then took us up the hill to the office of the one in charge of the border. He graciously welcomed us with tea, candies, nuts, sweets, and water-melon. We shared the delightful camaraderie of friends under fire.

I felt joyfully at home again among the Uzbek-speaking soldiers who guard the border. Even the one Pashtun officer in charge speaks fluent Uzbek. He is one of the finest examples I've known of a Pashtun who will have nothing to do with the Taliban. For years he has been one of the loyal lieutenants for Mawmir Hasan, the respected Uzbek commander of Dasht-e Qaleh.

His hospitality to us that night was unforgettable. It reminded me that it's often not what you know but who you know that matters. I experienced again the Afghan principle of reciprocity. Even though I know it isn't true, as the person identified with all the relief that flows into the area of DQ, I often sense that others feel indebted to me. On that night, I was so glad that they felt it was their turn to offer assistance and return favors. We were certainly in need of their help that night. All the blood, sweat, tears, and hard work had built an invisible bridge of friendship that brought us across that river. God truly provides, sometimes in the most surprising ways, for those who faithfully serve the poor.

That same month, Afghanistan saw continual action on the front lines to our west. Although we were several miles away, the sounds of war were always with us. At night, the battle noises seemed louder—so much louder we often couldn't sleep. We sometimes climbed onto our rooftop in Nowabad and sat in stunned silence watching rocket fire and tracer bullets light up the horizon. These were not the friendly fireworks of freedom that I had celebrated just the month before at home in the U.S. In fact, their sights and sounds were gruesome reminders of the daily, dismal destruction of Afghanistan.

PUBLIC SANITATION PROJECTS

I returned to Afghanistan anxious to see the progress that had been made on several of our work efforts. As with most of the projects I have supervised in Afghanistan, this one has a personal connection. Because I travel widely in the Dasht-e Qaleh area, I am rarely at home for bathroom breaks. We have a very nice latrine in the

Nowabad compound that I am seldom able to use. My frequent visits to Khvajeh Baha od Din highlighted this problem. When I first arrived in town, a bamboo mat wrapped around a couple of sticks served as the only private location for outsiders to take care of bodily needs.

Eventually we built an eight-stall public latrine in Khvajeh Baha od Din. The people in town readily agreed to the construction and worked alongside our engineer. They saw the value of this sanitation project. It became a mark of the town's hospitality that they provided such a facility for visiting strangers. My first opportunity to use the facilities turned out to be a memorable occasion.

Outside the newly constructed latrine, a little elderly Uzbek man had seized the entrepreneurial moment. He set up a small table to provide bottles of water for wash up and squares of excellent, soft, pink toilet paper to those using the latrine. I laughed with delight as I handed him my ten cents for the basic necessities. It reminded me of the ingenuity of American children, who set up lemonade stands in the summer.

In many communities in Afghanistan, the marginal sanitation poses serious health risks. Waste from larger animals, like cows, is left to dry and used as fuel, but human waste gets recycled in less than picturesque ways. Odor frequently adds to the problem too. At this stage, disease is just around the corner. These factors usually show up in the worst way in towns that have a crowded open-air market. Once word got out about the wonderful public latrine in Khvajeh Baha od Din, we also had to build one in Rostaq, Yangi Qala, and Chah Ab.

Our concern went far beyond *public* sanitation, though. We knew that a key factor in making the DQ Host Family Program work depended on our ability to equip living compounds with well-constructed latrines. We believe that the quality of life inside Afghanistan has definitely been improved by these health-care measures.

Shelter for Life and other NGOs have helped people in northern Afghanistan build thousands of latrines. These are often the result of community-wide projects. Neighbors help each other dig the containment pits, frame and pour the base, and construct the walls and roof. The synergy that flows from this teamwork often promotes other community projects.

The Yaftal Latrine Project stands out as a great example of the multiplied effects created by such a basic upgrade on village homes. The initial project proposal called for the construction of four hundred thirty latrines in the poorer villages of Yaftal Payan. Alongside the building aspects, we planned a series of community education opportunities. As an added incentive, due to the extreme impact of the drought, we planned to give one hundred sixty kilograms of wheat to each family that completed their latrines. Most of the residents in these villages had been devastated by the drought. This food-for-work plan would offer the community a win-win situation. As sanitation and health conditions improved, dysentery and disease would recede. As wheat was given and ground to flour, hunger pains would disappear as people ate daily bread.

I met with the respected local commander of Yaftal, who designated the villages to receive the materials for the latrines. We then sent two of our native staff members to survey the families in those villages in order to identify which ones were most in need of the project's assistance.

During the summer of 2001, we were ready to provide rebar and cement to the participants. We launched the construction phase of the project in early June. Our proposal estimated the job would take three months. But the last of the structures was in use in just over two months. A combination of the people's enthusiasm and cooperation and our staff's effective management and supervision resulted in successful implementation and speedy completion.

Because of increased pressure on supply lines by the Taliban, the UN experienced severe shortages of shipped-in wheat and other supplies. Logistical difficulties multiplied. Even money was in short supply due to lack of travel to and from Islamabad, Pakistan. At this point, the WFP owed cash payments to almost every truck driver in northern Afghanistan. Some of our distributions depended on my own purchase of barrels of diesel to fuel the trucks delivering wheat.

The rapid conclusion of the Yaftal project meant that those involved looked forward to the promised wheat payments. We had to give them partial wheat allowances and promises of more wheat later. When we distributed those first four hundred and thirty 50-kilogram bags of wheat, I had no idea just how much the world would change in the next month before I returned with the remainder of hard-earned food for work.

TURNING POINT

September 2001 arrived. I had been inside the country almost a year. With God's help, much good had been done. But the war sounds in the background constantly reminded me of how little had really changed. There seemed no end to the suffering. All around me in the darkness of the village were people whose lives had been ripped apart by the fighting. Their homes were gone. Family members were missing or dead. The explosions in the distance seemed to mock my helplessness and insignificance.

Standing again on our flat roof in Nowabad, I felt a rising tide of frustration inside. I found myself once more weeping for the people I was trying to help. Overwhelmed with the circumstances around me, I cried out to God, instinctively raising my hands and my eyes upward. As my head tilted back, it was as if my tears acted like added lenses for my eyes, and I saw the night sky in a new way. The diamond stars seemed magnified and brilliant. I was drawn into the awesome wonder of God's universe. I felt wrapped in the power of the one who, with just an almighty word, made all that I could see and so much more. I was overwhelmed with God's greatness.

Under that amazing display of stars, I thought of another man, many centuries ago, looking up at the same sky, not so far from where I was standing. Abram was his name. He's now known to billions as Prophet Abraham, the father of Judaism, Christianity, and Islam. God promised him that his offspring would number as many as the stars in the heavens. He also told Abraham that all the families of the earth would be blessed through him. And I thought, *When and how will this come to Afghanistan?* Then I wondered if my being here had even a tiny part in God's divine plan of great blessing.

I cried out in prayer again to God, "Please have mercy, for if someone doesn't bring an end to this war, this country is in deep trouble."

RICOCHET!

The possibility of General Massoud's assassination had hung over Afghanistan, like the threatening blade of a guillotine, for a long time. We all knew the Taliban and Al Qaeda would have rejoiced to see him dead. Osama bin Laden's hatred toward the Lion of the Panjshir ran deep. In fact, many attempts had been made on his life, and he had faced several close calls in battle. Even so, his murder on September 9 shocked and horrified us all. It was just a small snapshot compared to the giant mural of dread and terror the greater suicide mission would paint the morning of 9/11.

By the time I awoke on the morning of September 12, I realized, in a dim way, that the aftermath of the dastardly explosion that killed General Massoud had ricocheted into every corner of the globe and set off a chain reaction that rocked the foundations of the world.

We could not have perfectly predicted the events of September 11, 2001, any more than our grandfathers could have clearly seen the coming of December 7, 1941. Prior to Japan's bombing of Pearl Harbor, it was obvious that the world was at war. It was already clear that at least Germany, Italy, and Japan stood united as enemies against the USA and other allied nations.

We knew the Axis coalition hated America with an unholy passion. And our presence in the Pacific Ocean was a serious barrier to their twisted scheme to make the world a better place through Nazism. We knew that America's superpower status posed a major threat to their ill-conceived plan to conquer the world. We also knew they had airplanes and other weapons of mass destruction at their command. Actually, it was the Japanese who made Kamikaze missions famous. These were military versions of what we call certain forms of suicide bombing today.

And yet, for someone to have said, "On the morning of December 7, 1941, the Japanese will launch an all-out attack at Pearl Harbor" would have taken the then-known facts and placed them into the mystic realm of fortune telling. Was it possible to predict an attack by Japan at some point? Absolutely. Was it possible to predict it perfectly on the day and time it happened? Not in my opinion. But now, as always, hindsight is twenty-twenty. If we focus on the results of that chain reaction in 1941, that evil event obviously launched our country into World War II. Yes, it was a terrible blow, and the war was extremely costly. Ultimately, though, we and our united allies brought down those wicked regimes and set the world upright again.

We must be careful, in my mind, when looking back at historical events (whether they were good or bad), not to think that we have the power to stop them at will. If our probing into the past is for more reasons than the desire to learn from those events, our intellectual pursuit may be useless. Wisdom tells us to learn from our mistakes in order to prepare ourselves for what the future may bring. It also tells us not to bash unjustly, blame blindly, or believe without reservation that the events of history can be completely controlled by the White House, FBI, and CIA.

The truth is, we live in a world that's full of both good and evil.

Yes, we must do all in our power to make the world a better place by promoting peace and fighting for freedom and justice. And we should improve our intelligence systems, tighten control at the border, and support the war on terrorism. But in our attempts to rid the world of Satan's influence, we must also embrace the truth that, though it's a noble goal worthy of blood, sweat, and tears, it's absolutely humanly impossible to fully carry it out to completion until the Prince of Peace comes again.

The Great Dilemma

September 12, 2001: A Bad Dream?

FEYZABAD—On the morning of September 12, 2001, unusual noises elsewhere in the building interrupted my sleep. A mixture of my friends' voices and the crackling of the shortwave radio rose and fell among the other sounds of the awakening city. I kept my eyes tightly closed. Nothing about this new day encouraged me to open them.

Gradually, certain words and phrases in the radio transmissions pulled back my curtain of sleepiness: "America is at war." "America has been attacked, and the enemy is about to feel the wrath of an angry superpower." "Lives have been lost and saved in the World Trade Center towers," and "the heroes of Flight 93." It was hard to make sense of any of it, because it felt so far away, in that semiconscious place somewhere between asleep and awake.

Finally, familiar words snapped open my eyelids, as if from a bad dream: "Osama bin Laden," "Al Qaeda," and "Afghanistan." Every story seemed to mention, in the same breath, my homeland and the land that I have called home for a year. Afghanistan had changed overnight from a little-known, blank spot on the globe to the center of world attention. I got my knees under me on the sleeping mat and stood up. I had work to do.

Radio reports repeatedly named bin Laden and his Al Qaeda network as the terrorists behind the 9/11 attacks. Since we couldn't see the horrid video footage or photographs of the ongoing nightmare, it was difficult to fully comprehend the shock that we heard in the voices of Americans being interviewed. For us, the attacks presented a new side to our immediate problem and a great dilemma. We had to decide whether to stay in Afghanistan or evacuate. We reacted to the broadcast news reports and the reality around us as well as we could. Several days later, I would weep in pain and astonishment as I watched the 9/11 footage for the first time.

EVACUATE OR STAY?

We talked with the Shelter for Life regional office in Tajikistan several times that day. Other supporting agencies participated in those discussions. Three of our team's six members were ordered to evacuate immediately. Their supporting agency had a security plan with a low tolerance for risk. We had already decided among ourselves the day before that an evacuation by *any* of us would probably mean an evacuation by *all* of us.

Sometime during the morning of September 12, we were surprised to hear the UN airplanes taking off. It took us a little while to verify that their entire staff had evacuated eastward to Pakistan. For one reason or another, we were not included in plan A. This left us one evacuation route, plan B—the border at Eshkashem. With half our group already ordered to leave the country, I had to make a personal decision that would affect the rest of the team. My heart was breaking and heavily burdened.

I was the only team member who had been to the Eshkashem border before. I knew from personal mistakes how complicated it could be to cross that border. I could at least take the group there. Two of the people with us didn't have valid Tajik visas, so there would have to be some tricky negotiations to get them into Tajikistan. And they needed me to translate.

As the day and the discussions wore on, I realized I really had no choice. It would be best for all of us to head to the border together. Once we reached that conclusion, the regional office simply settled matters by asking us all to leave the country. They told us that someone from Dushanbe would travel down to Eshkashem with the paperwork to allow the pair of "illegals" to cross into Tajikistan.

By the time all these decisions were made, it was too late in the day to start our trek to the Tajik border, so we planned our departure for early the next morning. The radio continued to feed us the heartbreaking news from home. Slowly the suffering and agony of the tragic events back in the States began to seep into our hearts and minds.

SORTING IT ALL OUT

We spent the remainder of the day delegating things at the office, packing, crying, praying, and talking. I was busy contacting all of our local staff and settling up our finances, in case we were prevented from returning right away. I wanted to leave with a clear conscience. Love makes a better memory than debt.

This meant changing several thousand dollars into barely manageable stacks of Afghanis. I delivered sacks of money to a couple of bakeries we had contracted to provide bread for local IDPs. I paid the rent on several buildings and gave our local staff their current salaries. By the end of the day, we owed nothing in northern Afghanistan but a debt of love for the people we came to serve. None of this diminished the feeling in me that I was abandoning my post.

As we tried to sort things out, in one way, everything we heard on international radio about the 9/11 attacks made sense. The events fit with our experience. General Massoud's assassination was one ugly piece of a worldwide puzzle of terror. My Afghan friends in the north took no joy in the evil that was done to America. They identified with our sorrow out of their own great loss. In fact, most were angry, ashamed, and embarrassed that the evil of September 9 and September 11 was done in the name of Allah.

As I talked to our local staff and assured them we planned to return, they were eager to express their sadness for my country. Several apologized.

"This is not our view of Islam or what is means to be a Muslim," one said. "We don't believe that evil suicide bombers, who kill innocent people in the name of Allah, go to paradise as a reward for their wickedness."

These men had become friends. They wanted to comfort me. One of them walked me back to the office, gripping my hand in a handshake while his arm held my shoulders. Our mutual tears mingled in the dust. I had no words to tell them how much harder their expressions of love made it for me to leave.

When night fell, we gathered at the office. Our bags were packed and ready for an early departure. We sat by lamplight and talked late into the night, trying to sort out our feelings and thoughts from the day. Several versions of the same question eventually dominated the discussion: Why would the Taliban and Al Qaeda, on the verge of taking control of all of Afghanistan, suddenly decide to enrage the world's remaining superpower? Why bomb America when their plans for Central Asia were making great progress? Why pick a fight with the biggest guy on the block when you can barely handle the fight you're already in? We guessed it had to be the result of arrogance, stupidity, and the will to destroy.

In the days before 9/11, we tried hard to figure out how soon more bad things would be happening in northern Afghanistan because of the Taliban and Al Qaeda. The terrorist training camps of bin Laden were growing and spreading. Time seemed to be on their side. One day later, the picture radically changed. The more we heard about the steely resolve in the U.S. to respond to the attacks, the more we realized that bad news was on its way to the Taliban and Al Qaeda.

As Americans, we soon began to compare the terrorist strikes with the only similar disaster in our history—Pearl Harbor. Like that infamous day of December 7, 1941, our hellish day of 9/11 would only serve to "wake a sleeping giant." I have since come to understand in a new way that sudden, inexplicable changes in human events are not accidents. They point to God's sovereign or complete control of his universe. The Bible reveals that God rules heaven and earth. I believed he would bring greater good out of these awful, evil events. Ultimately God's plan of justice makes every wrong right. These terrorist attacks and our response to them no doubt fit into a bigger picture, even though our view of it is not crystal clear.

To Eshkashem Again

Early the next morning, our local staff sent us on our way. They had already performed their first Muslim prayers for the day, but they stood quietly in the chill with us as we prayed for their safety. We all held out our empty hands to ask the Creator of the world to kindly watch over us all. Then we shook hands all around, with our left hands resting on our hearts and our right hands reaching out for one another.

"Salaam Alekkum," we softly exchanged, looking into each other's eyes. *"Khudo khafis,"* which literally means "God protect you" were the last tearful words we spoke that day. We didn't know if we would ever meet again.

The six of us shoehorned ourselves into two Afghan-driven Russian Jeeps. Our road trip took us through snowcapped mountains and peaceful valleys that we couldn't enjoy because of our heavy hearts. I tried to point out some of the history I had learned on my trip through this area nine months earlier, but none of us was really interested.

Things at the border looked unchanged from my previous visit. The dirt road that left Eshkashem gave no indication that it led to an international crossing. A small shack and a wired gate marked the Afghan side of the border. A simple bridge spanned the river. The familiar boxcarlike container that housed the Tajik and Russian personnel sat on the far shore. Getting *out* of Afghanistan was easy. The border guards had little interest in keeping people in the country.

Entering Tajikistan, though, proved a bit more complicated. I left the rest of the group in the relative protection of the Jeeps and began to negotiate. After each round, I ran back to my group to confer. I quickly lost ground. When the guards discovered that the six of us only had four visas between us, they began to shake their heads. We also wanted to bring a Jeep purchased in Afghanistan with us into the country. This news brought even more negative responses from our border friends. I got tired of running back and forth, fighting the cutting wind and eating the dust it continually kicked up. A difficult day was again developing for me at this unfavorable border crossing.

By now the sun had run its course. Hours of hard work and juggling various dialects hadn't impressed the border guards. They shrugged and told us it was too late. We would have to return to the Afghan side, and quickly, before the guards on that side locked the gate and went home. If that happened, we would just have to spend in the night in no-man's-land between the two countries. Things were coming down to the wire.

I had been quietly insisting, in my simple Tajik, "In the name of the Lord, we will all cross together with the vehicle." They all laughed every time I said it. After all, we might be Americans and other foreigners, but this was the Tajik border out in the middle of nowhere, and they were in charge.

Finally our friend arrived from Dushanbe with the proper papers for the couple that had no visas. He also brought some Pepsi Cola to share with the guards. That simple gesture broke the international crisis. The six-hour-long standoff ended. They suddenly allowed us into the country with one final condition—we had to give them a ride into town before we went on our way. One minute the door was closed; the next it swung open. We had no doubt that God had made a way for us when no way seemed possible.

I MUST GO BACK!

DUSHANBE—Once we were in Tajikistan, we had an eighteen-hour drive ahead of us to our destination. We were exhausted when we reached Dushanbe on September 15. I was glad that we all arrived safely, but I was convinced that I should return to Afghanistan, alone if necessary. I had been dragging my feet all the way from Feyzabad. However, it was nice to have a break, to take a shower, go to church, and visit with friends in the big city. But after a week, I was anxious to return to the land that I now loved. I thought, *I must go back, because I left most of my heart there.*

I began to discuss with our regional director, Mark Baltzer, how I might get back inside Afghanistan. He thought I needed to wait. One of the immediate concerns about my returning had to do with Americans being in the country if the U.S. military bombed it. Much of the work that we had done in northern Afghanistan had involved the application of funding and materials, like USAID wheat, that had originated from the States. No one knew how American bombs would be received. Afghans have a history of setting differences aside in the face of a perceived common enemy. Would the Northern Alliance welcome our involvement?

There were also questions about how my presence in Afghanistan might be perceived by all sides. However, I thought everyone's overly cautious concern could paralyze us and keep us from responding with God's compassion to the poor and suffering. Potential danger may cause some to worry, but for others it creates a wonderful work atmosphere in which to practice faith and self-less service.

I respectfully but persistently explained my point of view. Things were developing rapidly as a result of 9/11, but there was little reason to believe that even if the U.S. launched attacks against Al Qaeda, that those would affect northeastern Afghanistan. The Northern Alliance showed no signs of buckling, and hopes were growing daily that America was gathering an international coalition that could mount a crushing blow to the Taliban and their allies. This hope was a cherished dream of the United Front or Northern Alliance, who remained in control of the areas where I worked.

On another side of the issue were international voices raised on behalf of the suffering in Afghanistan. If foreign forces attacked Afghanistan, would that not worsen conditions even more? Dire warnings about the terrible winter coming and the prospects of thousands of starving refugees seemed to complicate the issue. Should the international community concentrate its efforts on wiping out the Taliban or on preserving the lives of the millions of suffering people in and around Afghanistan?

From my perspective, we certainly weren't doing all we could. There were plenty of opportunities to help people in the northern area, and I was itching to get back in there. This was exactly the kind of situation where I wanted to serve. I was wired for this very moment. I felt like a freshman football player who keeps jumping off the bench and begging, "Come on, send me in, Coach!"

By now it had become clear that, while many of the terrorists who had attacked my country had been trained in Afghanistan, no Afghan had directly participated in that cowardly act. I felt no animosity at all toward the people of Afghanistan. I couldn't get over the genuine expressions of sadness and solidarity I had received from my Afghan friends. They had already suffered for such a long time, yet they expressed such great sorrow over the loss of life in America. Or, perhaps, *because* of their losses, they could empathize with us. They were ashamed that those claiming to be Muslims did such an unholy act. I knew that their suffering wasn't over, but neither was my responsibility to help wherever I could.

In Dushanbe, I saw on Russian and Tajik television stations a few news clips of the actual attack against the World Trade Center. I also saw some pictures on the Internet that gave me a deeper appreciation for what my fellow Americans had been and were going through. My heart was crushed and broken every time I saw the news. At times, I sat and wept uncontrollably. Naturally I wanted to help in some way back home. But I realized from brief, direct phone contacts with my family that the way I could probably do the most good would be to return to the place where I had already been serving. Thousands of Americans from across the country were rushing to help and serve at the tragic sites back home. But now, no one was rushing to help the still-bruised and bleeding people of Afghanistan. I knew I had to stay.

IF GOD OPENS THE DOOR . . .

After long conversations and prayer, my boss, Mark, gave me permission to seek a possible entrance into Afghanistan. The UN had abandoned all flights for fear of being shot down. All the borders were officially closed. I knew from past experience that officially closed borders could often be unofficially opened. The conditions from our office were clear: If God opened the door into the country, I was permitted to go through it. The rest they left up to my discretion, diligence, and determination.

Flying in Tajikistan can be a high-risk experience, especially the route between Dushanbe and Khorugh. Pilots get paid extra because they have to clear the Hindu Kush range in less than prime aircraft and then land between mountains. It's so close you can almost reach out the windows and touch the snow-tipped mountain peaks. If visibility isn't perfect, the planes don't take off from Dushanbe. The airline should be called Wing-and-a-Prayer Air.

The first minor miracle occurred when I went to the Dushanbe airport the morning of September 24. Again I heard the Tajik phrase, "If the sky is soft we will fly." On that day, the heavens were clear, and I took the flight from Dushanbe to Khorugh. My recent eighteen-hour driving ordeal suddenly shrank to a one-hour flight. That put me just sixty miles north of the same border at Eshkashem that I had crossed only eleven days before.

At the local bazaar, I made arrangements with a Tajik man to drive me to the border. While we ate lunch, I tried to explain the time constraints related to the border. He nodded that he understood, but his pace remained unchanged. In Central Asia, life does not move to the tick of the clock. They are much more event oriented and group minded. We may think we understand this, but when we're in a hurry, we quickly demonstrate that we don't. Needless to say, the driver stopped by his house on the way out of town to fill his wife in on his plans. Since I was probably an important figure to him, I had to be introduced to everyone in his family. I was trying my best not to be the ugly American wearing the demanding Timex watch, but I desperately wanted to get going.

Once we left Khorugh, things started moving like clockwork. But not for long. We stopped every so often to pick up someone along the road. Tajik hospitality began to wear on me. My driver also had a maddening fuel-saving technique. He turned off his engine and coasted down miles of twisting mountain roads. He would let the car coast almost to a complete stop before throwing it back into gear.

Then, as if to add insult to delay, we also had a flat tire. The driver remembered a distant relative who lived nearby. I tried to keep my sarcastic outlook to myself. How could anyone in such an isolated place help us? To my surprise, not only did the man actually exist, he even had the right-sized tire on a rim he was willing to give us. Another miracle! As we drove on, I realized that it was time to practice some patience.

The KGB border office was closed when I arrived late that afternoon. According to the remaining officials and soldiers, I had just missed the Russian border forces. When they learned that my plan was to cross into Afghanistan, they were not pleased. In fact, it didn't appear that they would give me permission. They kept repeating insistently, "This border is closed."

AN UNEXPECTED ALLY

ESHKAMESH—I had no choice but to retrace my steps a few miles to the main KGB office of Eshkamesh. At first I was treated as if I had already done something wrong. Thankfully, when the ranking Russian official arrived, he acted more favorably. In fact, he said that I could stay in the KGB office overnight, and in the morning he would personally take me to the border.

We had a stimulating conversation that evening. His questions seemed motivated by genuine personal curiosity rather than official duty. He showed interest in our work in Tajikistan, as well as Afghanistan. He offered me one of the beds for lodging and then served me eggs, bread, and tea for breakfast. He also proved to be an expert in international relations. I was reminded of a simple rule of thumb I have repeatedly found to be true: *Where God guides, he also provides.* I expressed my gratitude for the official's kindhearted help.

That morning, when we drove to the border, one of the Russian guards remembered me from our recent departure.

"America! America!" he greeted me as I climbed out of the

vehicle. He was a big guy who looked like the Russian boxer in the film *Rocky*. He was, no doubt, pro-American.

HOME AGAIN!

AFGHANISTAN—The crossing went smoothly. Just a few minutes later, I was back inside Afghanistan. Our Dushanbe office had contacted one of our national staff members in Feyzabad, so one of our vehicles was waiting for me on the other side.

What a joy to be back! So much had changed in less than two weeks. I enjoyed the ride and a time of "catching up" with our driver and one of our project supervisors. We arrived at our office and were warmly greeted by the rest of our staff. At that point, it first occurred to me that I was probably the only American left in northern Afghanistan. In fact, I may have been the only international staff person for any of the relief agencies in that part of the country. I definitely had my work cut out for me.

On September 26, 2001, I visited the familiar UN-WFP office just down the dusty road from us. Yes, the news was true, they informed me. None of the international staff of the UN agencies had returned yet. But the local staff was eager and willing to help. We chatted like old friends and then turned our combined attention to our immediate plans.

I had a long to-do list. The first item involved a request for 860 fifty-kilogram bags of wheat for our project in Yaftal. The Latrine Project in the drought-affected villages of Yaftal had been completed, but we had been able to deliver only the first third of the wheat-for-work payments, due to shortages and lack of transportation.

On September 28, I traveled with four big trucks loaded with USAID wheat up to Yaftal. We had told the people the day before to come to the designated distribution point. When we arrived, hundreds of donkeys and people anxiously awaited some hard-earned food. I was greeted as if I were the king of Persia and instantly served watermelon by a group of Northern Alliance soldiers, who came to help with crowd control.

At that time, just a couple of weeks after 9/11, the American-led air strikes were imminent. However, the soldiers and our beneficiaries asked no questions about my nationality. I had 860 bags of goodwill with me. They were too happy about getting food to ask, and I was too overjoyed with the privilege of serving them to mention it. That distribution was one of the most peaceful days of my life.

THE NIGHT VISITOR

FEYZABAD—The night before I left Feyzabad I had an unexpected visitor at the office. Local authorities, from fear of the unknown, were now asking people to stay home after dark for their own safety, and they enforced a strict curfew. Someone knocking on my door in the dark obviously didn't understand that law enforcement in northern Afghanistan usually shoots first and asks questions later.

When I opened the door, I was face to face with another American. We exchanged names, which turned out to be slightly comic, because his name is also John. He was a journalist with the *New Yorker*. He had received news that there was still an American humanitarian in the area with SNI/Shelter for Life, and he wanted to see if it was true.

He asked, "John, are you the only American aid worker here in the country right now?"

I replied, "Perhaps, but I don't know for sure." We didn't talk long, and I declined any official interview. I didn't think anyone else needed to know where I was at the time. But his interest reminded me that the world's eye was suddenly on Afghanistan. I didn't imagine that soon hundreds of journalists like John would be in my neighborhood.

THE ROAD TO ROSTAQ

The following day, I left Feyzabad for Rostaq. I needed to get to our central field office to pay all our monthly bills and salaries. Since it was also the end of the month, I could help our Afghan accountant close our September 2001 books.

We also were about to receive some more WFP wheat for the workers laboring on our fifty-kilometer mountain road from Rostaq to DQ. I anticipated seeing the progress of the road after a month's absence. Many on those work crews had become personal friends. It would also be sweet to present USAID wheat to Afghans, when so many in the world were either expressing feelings of hatred towards Muslims or accusing America of anti-Islamic actions.

Driving the road to Rostaq, I remembered my first trip across those rough miles. Not much had changed in a year. In the distance was the military junkyard known as the airport. Burned-up fields and dry land reminded me of the continued drought. The mountains still offered the same mute-but-magnificent witness to God's omnipotence. The roads were full of donkeys and the taste of heat and dust. The people looked the same. But everything seemed more familiar to me. This place was my home, even if not my homeland.

This September there was a sense of hope in the air. Many thought that the evil of 9/11 would result in greater good. For the average Afghan citizen, this meant the downfall of the Taliban. Of course, no one was dancing with joy at the thought of U.S. air strikes. Reality said that some innocent civilians could be casualties. The country would, no doubt, experience more damaging blows as bombs and missiles leveled homes and buildings. But the cry of thousands of refugees was for justice, liberty, and freedom from the tyranny of the Taliban. The greater reality was that, if America did not respond, millions of Afghans wouldn't have a prayer for survival. An all-out war on terrorism was their only hope.

Ambassador for God

I must say that it was a privilege to be in Afghanistan, whether or not I was the only active American relief worker. Whether I was safe or not, I felt secure. Whether I lived or died, I knew I was right where God wanted me to be. I reminded myself that many people, who were praying for me, would join me if they could.

My return communicated a powerful message to our local staff and those we were serving: *We really care about you. We care enough to stay when the going gets tough.* My presence in the country was not about me or my desires or my great plan. Instead, it was all about God's apparent choice in letting me return to Afghanistan as one of his ambassadors. I felt privileged to be on this mission of mercy, serving the wonderful people of Afghanistan.

Invasions

AFGHANISTAN—Before the U.S.-led military strikes against the Taliban and Al Qaeda in Afghanistan began, another massive group mounted an invasion of their own. An army of journalists and media workers overran the borders to cover the assassination of General Massoud and the imminent war on terrorism.

The little town of Khvajeh Baha od Din, several miles east of my house in Nowabad, turned into the mecca of media. The terrorist attack of September 9 that killed General Massoud had occurred there. The United Front or Northern Alliance also had its military headquarters and the Ministry of Foreign Affairs office in Khvajeh Baha od Din. This small village of a few thousand families instantly became the host to hundreds of journalists. And too many story-hungry reporters in extremely close quarters created a great deal of confusion.

It was amazing to witness the flood of westerners coming to where I had recently been the only American. They all congregated in this dusty area of northeastern Afghanistan, because the Taliban still controlled 90 percent of the country. All the main borders were closed to westerners; but the northeast, or Massoud's and Rabbani's domain, remained open to the outside world. The two provinces of

Badakhshan and Takhar didn't provide enough news stories to satisfy the ravenous appetite of the worldwide media.

This nosy new presence had a direct impact on our work for many reasons. First, I had to work hard at avoiding the media, or I could not get my work done. I'm sure I could have become a twenty-four-hour instant celebrity if I had wanted . . . but I *didn't* want that.

I remember the first time I saw the milling herd of journalists. I had gone to Khvajeh Baha od Din to exchange some money and buy supplies. I fit in well as an Afghan with my native dress, beard, and passable speech so I was not recognized. But it was obvious they were in town and spending money left and right, because the value of the U.S. dollar had dropped to half its former worth.

I remember feeling cheated and thinking, *These journalists with their big budgets are messing up the economy for those of us who will stay here and work after they drive off in the dust looking for another sound bite.*

The journalists were walking everywhere with their expensive cameras, camcorders, and microphones. They were paying one hundred dollars a day for a translator and a hired driver. One hundred dollars *each* per day—about the average monthly salary for the local Afghans who worked with an NGO in order to serve their own people. As an American, I was embarrassed by my countrymen flaunting their western wealth in the faces of the world's destitute and poor. And since America's affluence is one of Osama bin Laden's battle cries, it was even more distasteful to me.

I remember the first time I was asked for an interview with one of the major networks. I had returned to Khvajeh Baha od Din and this time I was spotted. A translator for one of the journalists saw me and said, "Mr. John!" My cover blown, I had to come face to face with a megamicrophone. The reporter asked if he could interview me because, as he said, "I need some sound bites."

"Why not?" I said, thinking that someone needed to tell the world the truth about the desperate situation around me. I don't think it's what he wanted to hear, though. His questions were centered on the plight of the refugees or displaced people he had seen in DQ and the surrounding countryside. He was shocked to learn that all those displaced families had lived in that area for over a year. They were not fleeing the imminent Allied air strikes. These families had been suffering for years because of the tyranny of the Taliban.

I tried to give him a crash course in the tragedies that occurred while the rest of the world slept. His surprise mounted as he learned that I, an American aid worker, had lived in this war zone longer than most of the IDPs. But my story clearly didn't fit the scheduled, predetermined news angle for that day. So he quickly lost interest and cut the interview short.

In general, I wasn't happy with the pushy journalists or their brash approaches in a world that was not used to westerners. Many of them did very little to educate themselves about their surroundings or the history of the situation. They were too busy spending money and getting comfortably set up, instead of uncovering the facts that the world desperately needed to hear.

I also remember thinking, *How sad that the most blessed nation in the world has to taste a terrorist attack before even noticing millions in Afghanistan, who have been suffering for years.*

However, my attitude did eventually change. Happily, my original assumptions turned out to be partly wrong. I actually had a few good media experiences, which started with a conversation with Charles Sennott from the *Boston Globe*. I hosted him as a guest for a few nights at our Nowabad (DQ) office. He was actually paying attention and taking notes. It was obvious, by his choice of questions, that he really wanted to learn.

One night he said, "John, it would really be great if someone did a piece on your work here. The world, especially Americans, need to know that you are here and doing such an awesome job of serving the Afghans who are displaced by the tyranny of the Taliban."

I thought it was a good idea but made no comment. However, Charles continued to pursue this plan until, finally, around the first of October, I let him write a *Boston Globe* article about our work.

A few days later, he talked to me about an ABC television interview with his friend David Wright. I was flattered but feeling that I had better things to do. I came here to serve, not to be a celebrity. Besides, we had lots of wheat to distribute that week. I didn't have time to stop for the interview. In fact, our four-room mud mansion didn't even have TV.

I eventually agreed to a taped interview, if the crew could find me, but I wasn't going to make any special efforts to accommodate them. They would have to take the initiative; I was just too busy. I told them they were welcome to come to our DQ office or accompany us to one of our projects or distributions. That way, I could continue what I came to do, which was to serve people in need.

Somewhat to my surprise, they took me up on the offer. And for most of a day, I had a camera crew with me, getting up close and personal with the Afghan people. Based on their tape from that day, millions of Americans got a report of our work in action on *ABC World News Tonight* with Peter Jennings.

Prior to this, my only camera exposure occurred with Saira Shah in the spring of 2001, when she stayed with us for a week. She was filming the award-winning Afghan documentary *Beneath the Veil*. Soon after the Allied attacks, Saira returned and included some of our work in her follow-up documentary. She and her TV crew spent a second week with us. We helped her with logistics and local contacts as time permitted. As a result, her reports and personal efforts have expanded our network of donors to the continued support of our service. The work of Shelter for Life was seen all over the world on the CNN report "Unholy War."

AIR STRIKES

As far as I remember, we first started hearing airplanes, other than the familiar Taliban jets, the first week of October. At first it was hard to tell if they were dropping bombs or blessings. At any rate, the Taliban suddenly met their worst nightmare in the form of F-15s, B-52s, and cruise missiles. It's no pleasant feeling, being awakened at three o'clock in the morning to the sounds of bombers and jets. That equipment made a much louder statement than the old Russian planes the Taliban used or the Northern Alliance helicopters that daily transported supplies and soldiers. We often felt the ground shake under us.

In our area of northern Afghanistan, I saw only a little of the heavy bombing. The most strategic spot within our view was the mountain range of Katakala. The Taliban used that vantage point to bombard DQ and Massoud's border crossing. With the roaring rockets and Taliban tanks blown off those hills by the Allies, our area was finally liberated.

The next closest strikes were in Taloqan, Kondoz, and around Mazar-e Sharif, to our west. Doomsday for the Taliban had finally dawned. Scared to death, they retreated in all directions, but most of them congregated in Kondoz. The effects of the bombing reached us almost immediately. Villages across the river sent word that the Taliban were gone. Within weeks of this new war on terrorism, the flow of IDPs through our area began to reverse. People started going home. It was a beautiful sight to me.

Still, it was really hard for me, being there with my Afghan staff who were wondering, *Did that American bomb just kill an innocent civilian or one of my own relatives?* However, in our minds and hearts, we knew there was no other way. The Taliban and Al Qaeda would have never surrendered. In fact, possessed by evil itself, they would have probably all become suicide bombers and killed more innocent victims along with themselves.

I'm not in favor of war, but I do believe that, at times, it's the only effective form of human justice. Sometimes God, who is just, holy, and all-loving, allows war to bring about peace and a long-term plan of greater good.

FOOD DROPS

Soon some of the same planes began dropping food, clothes, and other types of assistance. I thought, *Where were you guys last year when we really needed you?*

These airdrops in our area were quite controversial. At first, the only recipients were soldiers and commanders. The drops were made at night, and therefore the soldiers were always the first to get there. They would shoot flares into the night sky to alert their comrades and then supervise their own distributions. What supplies the soldiers couldn't use often showed up for sale in the bazaar. I walked by stalls in the market with shelves stacked full of boxes that were clearly stenciled, "A GIFT FROM THE PEOPLE OF THE UNITED STATES."

These developments so disturbed me that I was determined to help in some way. I scolded some of my commander friends and said, "How can you expect God to bless your country when you rob the poor?" Most of them listened.

Refugees and neighbors came by and asked, "Mr. John, why don't you do something?"

They clearly assumed I had a hot line to the president or direct contact with the planes. After all, they thought, what the planes were dropping probably belonged to me. I was the only American there on the ground. I was "Mr. Distribution" who "did not fear anyone but God."

I wanted so badly to help that I said, "If I hear the planes again in the morning, I'll come and check it out."

I had heard stories about fights and even killings at these early-morning, in-the-dark distributions of airplane-dropped assistance. The sudden bounty dropped into the midst of poverty and despair sometimes brought out the worst in people.

One cold morning around three-thirty, I heard the planes making food drops. I rose from my sleep and hesitantly cranked up our motorcycle. I headed out on a cold, dark, desert trail of a highway to find the unknown point of distribution.

As I traveled, people and donkeys occasionally loomed out of the gloom. They were all amazed to see me.

Many of them shouted, "Mr. John, what are you doing?"

They wondered why I, the "rich American," would need to go and get free stuff from the airplanes. I stopped occasionally to ask about the drops. Hundreds were out roaming the darkness with me, and they confirmed that drops had occurred, but they had not found the landing spot yet.

After an hour and many miles on the chilling ride, I decided to give up. I stopped to greet some friends I recognized. I told them I was finished for the night and heading back to the office.

They said, "We think the drop was on the other side of Khvajeh Baha od Din."

I learned later that they were right. My attempt to bring order to the chaos of a night distribution turned out to be unsuccessful . . . and even painful.

Disappointed, I zoomed off into the darkness, looking forward to a hot cup of tea at the office. Soon I missed a turn and lost my way. Trail riding in the dark almost always includes detours. The moonless, starless night contributed to my endangered status. My headlight cast such a small pool of light in front of the bike that it was almost useless. And I wasn't experienced enough as a rider to realize the hazards of what I was doing. But I soon learned a valuable lesson. My front wheel sandwiched into a small ditch just off the narrow path and the cycle came to a jarring stop.

I took flight shortly before four-thirty that morning. I know what time it was, because my watch stopped when I landed. The takeoff was fast and smooth, but the landing was hard and rough; I ate dirt for breakfast. I realized that my mouth was cut and bleeding. My instincts told me to stand up, but when I tried, I fell back down. Then I passed out cold.

I might still be there, but one of my motorcycle buddies from DQ was behind me and heard me leave the road. He knew my ride through the scrub brush would shortly come to an end. It didn't take him long to find me. The headlight did its only good work for the night, creating a beacon for my helper to follow.

My friend picked me up and took me back to our office on my own motorcycle. Though I set out that night to be the Good Samaritan, one ending up saving me. I was sore from head to toe, and I thought I had a concussion or severe neck injury. Later that day, I felt even worse and could hardly move. But I rested and by the grace of God gradually healed. We even fixed the motorcycle for just over one hundred dollars.

One direct impact of all the air strikes is somewhat hard for me to put into words. It's another one of those overwhelming feelings I had one day about two months after 9/11.

During much of 2001, we served thousands of displaced families in Dasht-e Qaleh. At its largest expanse, the Nowabad camp had looked like a small tent city. Now, one day in November stands out vividly in my mind.

I drove down the mountainous road from Rostaq on a glorious and crisp winter day. One spot on the road allowed me to glimpse most of the camp at one time. On this day, I could see nothing. But etched in my mind was the horrible day a year ago when this same view overlooked three thousand blue tarps.

Now, the faded pathways and worn vegetation marked the location of the camp, but it was empty. The displaced crowds that had gathered around the distribution trucks were gone. The kids who climbed on the rusted Russian tank had left their toys and gone home. I began to cry.

Because of the war on terrorism and, therefore, the collapse of the Taliban's evil regime, tens of thousands of displaced Afghan families had been able to return to their original homes. This alone has changed our work drastically—for the better.

Now we have the privilege of helping these families resettle. We're providing the assistance they need to rebuild their lives, their homes, and their hopes for a better future. Thousands of families suffered for years because of the Taliban and its connection with Al Qaeda. The good news is that they have all been able to journey back to the places of their birth or to their own villages. There's no place like home. And all the fifteen thousand IDP families (over seventy-five thousand people), who were in our area of north-eastern Afghanistan, are no longer displaced or homeless. They are no longer in the open. They are home.

I couldn't hold back my tears as I saw the place that had consumed a year of my life and emotion. I was so glad they didn't need me anymore. Nowabad is the place where I was threatened as a doer of good, the place where I had lost sleep because of the suffering, and the place where I had the unique privilege of learning that it really is "more blessed to give than to receive." This area, where I daily smelled the stench of war, felt the sting of death, and saw the awful results of terrorism, had turned into a reminder of hope and peace. The place where babies cried and where people sometimes went to bed hungry or cold had become a place in my life that now stood for the victory of good over evil. Justice had come for the oppressors, and the people were free from the clutches of tyranny.

The camp was empty, like a ghost town. I was moved as I relived the last year of my life and how God had allowed me the privilege to work with SNI/Shelter for Life alongside an Afghan staff who were with me in helping to save the lives of so many. We often worked twelve hours a day, seven days a week, to serve, to help, to give, to do all we could do to avoid a major humanitarian crisis. We were able to share God's love on the front line.

From the shoulder of the mountain road, I could see our compound's mud walls glowing in the sun. That simple place funneled life to people. I stared at the roof where I had watched the bombings by Taliban jets and saw their rockets and missiles fly. I saw myself lift my hands to heaven and ask God to be merciful.

God shed his grace on this place in ways I could never have expected. I was filled with gratefulness, not only to God, but to so many others who have helped me get to that place where I could help those in need. Throughout my time in Afghanistan, I have been deeply aware that I am the last in a chain of people who pass on something good to others. I am grateful to DARE International in the UK for this partnership and for allowing me to work with SNI/Shelter for Life. Thanks to the Red, White, and Blue (to USAID/OFDA) that funded our emergency relief projects. And thanks to God for choosing me and putting me in the place of my dreams, a place to give my life to serve others. How grateful we all were that the war on terrorism brought justice and freedom to those who were oppressed.

MOVING TO SERVE

TALOQAN—Because all the IDP families left, many of the NGOs moved west from Feyzabad to Taloqan, the capital of Takhar. I remember that my first trip in that direction for a coordination meeting included numerous discoveries. When we arrived in the city, I was startled to see paved roads, big stores, large fruit-and-vegetable stands, and even some signs of electricity. What a jump in time from my little village of Nowabad. I was thrilled to drive on real roads. In comparison with the area in which I had lived and worked my first year in Afghanistan, I felt like a little kid from the farm going to the state fair for the first time.

However, the greatest feeling was actually seeing all our IDP friends moving back home. Everyone seemed to be headed in the same direction. They were on donkeys, camels, horses, and tractors, moving back into their villages in Takhar and Kondoz. I was overwhelmed when I saw so many friends in freedom, in peace, and in great joy as they journeyed home.

Trials and tribulations continue to challenge these devastated and damaged people. We all had to cross a river to get to the Taloqan section of Takhar. The bridge had been destroyed in the fighting. The area where we forded had gotten so much use that it became a quagmire with an appetite for vehicles. We almost lost our Jeep in the mud, but a tractor showed up with a cable and helped us cross. The IDPs around us were on a mission. I could see it in the way they walked. They no longer moved with the apathetic shuffle of the homeless. They moved with the determined steps of the homeward bound.

Watching them go moved me to tears. I had an idea of what awaited them: ruined wells, destroyed mosques, burned roofs, leveled buildings, demolished schools, and areas that had been mined by the Taliban or because of previous wars. There's no place like home, but theirs needed a lot of rebuilding. So much work was left to do. Thankfully, by this time, other organizations were on the scene to help.

SAMARITAN'S PURSE

The news about our presence in Afghanistan brought various organizations to our doors after 9/11. Millions of people were praying, and many were ready to help in tangible, practical ways. Spreading God's love through acts of compassion and missions of mercy is something we all can do.

One such group that quickly became our partner was Samaritan's Purse. This agency, led by Dr. Billy Graham's son, Franklin, carries out relief and development projects to benefit people all over the world. One of their best-known programs involves the packing of shoe boxes with practical and delightful gifts. Individuals, families, and churches pack millions of these shoe boxes every year. Samaritan's Purse delivers them to the forgotten children of the world.

While the agency has been welcomed in the majority of the nations of the world, they had never been able to take shoe boxes into Afghanistan. That became Franklin Graham's personal goal after the events of 9/11. His organization contacted our SFL/Dushanbe office with their plans and asked me to assist them with local arrangements. Shipments of large cardboard boxes stamped "Samaritan's Purse/ Operation Christmas Child" began to fill our storage space. Each one was filled with individual shoe boxes wrapped in colorful paper.

One of the greatest events of my life was actually assisting in the very first Operation Christmas Child shoe-box distribution in Afghanistan. What a day to remember for the students at our DQ school in December 2001, just a little over three months after the attacks on our country.

God orchestrated an amazing border crossing at the Amu Darya River for Gary Lundstrom and the Samaritan's Purse team. He used our history of faithfulness in service to not only smooth the way but also "build a bridge at the border." We made it to the school just in the nick of time. Soon the local leaders and all the teachers in DQ joined us in this amazing event.

We gathered all the first- through sixth-grade students, both boys and girls. More than eight hundred kids participated in this joyous celebration. We told them a little about Christmas and the idea that we imitate God's giving the greatest gift of all by giving gifts to one another.

We also explained the events of 9/11 to the students and

informed them that the children and families of the victims of the World Trade Center attacks packed many of the shoe boxes they were about to open. Some of these presents were sent in loving memory of firefighters, who lost their lives in New York trying to save the lives of others.

The Uzbek governor, Saed Sadek, who lost his home in Khvajeh Ghar because of the Taliban, was there to help us. I spoke in Dari, and he translated and reinforced my words in perfect Afghani Uzbek. Everyone was moved when they heard how the victims of 9/11 wanted to express God's love for the Afghan people.

Tears streamed down my face when I explained to a boy who had been orphaned by the Taliban that his present was from another orphan who became one because of the terrorist attacks of 9/11. He joined in my crying as he heard those words. It was quite an emotional day and clearly illustrated how the teachings of Jesus the Messiah truly promote peace, grace, and real forgiveness.

What an unforgettable sight to watch so many smiling, happy, joyful kids as they opened their Christmas boxes. No doubt, for many of them, these were the first real presents they had ever opened. I watched a little girl cautiously open her box. Nestled among assorted items lay a lovely dark-skinned doll that looked like her. She sat there very still as the chaos of joy swirled around her. I couldn't take my eyes off hers. They shone with a quality I can only describe as sheer wonder. She gently lifted the little figure out of the box and held it before her, taking in every detail. Then she wrapped the doll in a tight embrace and sat there rocking, eyes closed, lost in her own world of contentment.

Crayons, socks, gloves, games, toothbrushes, combs, hair bows, dolls—the assortment of gifts had the kids laughing with delight. The school erupted into spontaneous expressions of excitement, fun, and freedom. The release was contagious. Adults were laughing and crying at the same time, and then laughing at each other. After all the sadness and heartache of their last few years, I wished many more days like these for the children of Afghanistan.

CHANGES

The whole atmosphere in our area has become different now. Even though we live in a torn and frail society, great peace comes when with the absence of the threat of war. Fear has been replaced with a feeling of freedom, hope, opportunity, and joy in the air.

I am still overwhelmed that God allowed all the displaced people in our area to go back home. In fact, I'm convinced that God himself enters into the world of human suffering. I certainly sensed his presence inside Afghanistan during those darkest hours. One way God shows his love is through our acts of compassion and kindness. And when we speak out for justice, promote peace, or serve the poor, God is there.

You don't have to be on the front line of earthly war to do these godly things. In truth, we're all on the front line of war against the Evil One in this world every single day, whether in Afghanistan, America, or any other place on earth.

HOMECOMING

On December 20, 2001, I left northern Afghanistan. The trip was not easy for many reasons, but I wanted to get home to the States and surprise my family for Christmas. I wanted to give my mom a hug and tell her in person that I loved her. All my family had worried and prayed for me during the months of uncertainty in Afghanistan. I also wanted to see what was going on in my home country.

However, simple plans in Afghanistan often involve surprising twists. After doing the Operation Christmas Child distribution, I finished all my work in our Shelter for Life office to prepare for a trip to the States. I participated in one more round of those heart-felt Afghan handshakes and good wishes. As always, I told my staff and friends I would return.

When we arrived at the Amu Darya border crossing, our plans were delayed. The motorized barge had broken down, and the dark water flowed swiftly at my feet, blocking my way. Staring at the water, I thought, *Will I spend another Christmas inside Afghanistan?*

One of the Afghan guards standing behind me cleared his throat. I glanced over my shoulder into the familiar eyes of the brave sailor who had rowed me across this river under enemy fire one night back in August. He pointed up the river without a word. There, perched on the river bank was a small bamboo raft.

I looked back at him and nodded. He laughed joyously as we headed for another adventure together. I felt a little like Tom Sawyer and Huckleberry Finn. I may have started home for Christmas on a bamboo raft, but I still got there on time.

It's All about Life

WASHINGTON D.C.—The first time I landed in America after September 11 triggered thoughts and emotions I still find hard to describe. I'm not sure what I expected, but I was surprised by the changes I found. Between my visit over the Fourth of July 2001 and my arrival for Christmas the same year, radical alterations had occurred in my homeland. I sensed deep wounds, fresh scars, and a new awareness of our uniqueness as a nation.

My flight itinerary listed Dulles International Airport as my arrival airport. I realized we were almost there, because just beyond the wingtips of our airliner two F-15 Air Force jets suddenly appeared to provide an escort. They absolutely bristled with weapons. And I knew they weren't there to welcome me. *Wartime tension in the United States,* I thought, *feels just like wartime tension in Afghanistan.* And I was very familiar with the feeling.

As I walked through the terminal, I couldn't help but notice the signs. "God bless America." "United we stand." "In God we trust." "Proud to be an American." I saw U.S. flags draped, wrapped, and worn everywhere. On the highway to my grandmother's house in McLean, Virginia, almost every car displayed some form of patriotism—flags flying from windows, bumper stickers, window stickers. My memories of Independence Day included much less open evidence of national pride or self-awareness. Less than six months had passed, but I now recognized more clearly the trait that I love best about my own country—a fierce sense that we have something fragile called freedom that is worth defending . . . with fighting, if necessary.

ENDLESS EMOTIONS

While these feelings and thoughts were fresh in my mind, I sat down to make a list of them as they came: "overwhelmingly blessed," "in awe and wonder," "consumed with gratitude," "silent and speech-less," "undeserving yet privileged," "extremely excited but seriously sober," "drawn back to our heritage and foundation," and "remembering our forefathers." I kept returning to the idea that our nation is no accident. It was born with as much pain and pride as a new baby and with as many hopes and dreams for the future. America is a nation with a purpose. She's a grand experiment in liberty.

The thought of the great men who, though not perfect, shaped our founding documents and institutions continues to amaze me. They formed our nation with an eye toward human limitations and the hand of Providence. Even heroes of our history such as Jefferson, Franklin, and Payne, though not professed Christians, believed the idea of divine destiny and a sovereign Creator.

I was struck in a fresh way with the fact that our founding fathers had such a profound understanding of God's crucial role in human affairs that they dared to design a system of government that didn't try to force a certain religious belief on its citizens. The vast majority of them not only feared God but also believed that Jesus is the Lord of heaven and earth. That fact reminded me that genuine faith comes from within, rather than being imposed from without, even by well-meaning authorities.

Of course, the authors of the Declaration of Independence made their share of personal mistakes, but I was more impressed by the truth for which they lived and died: "One nation, under God, indivisible, with liberty and justice for all." Freedom includes, among other benefits, room for error or failure, endless choices and opportunities, individual decision and expression, and ultimately, the means to find faith.

I thought about how fortunate we are as a nation. Until Americans live elsewhere, we are prone to take so much for granted. We have a president, a government, and a constitution that serve the good of all under the rule of law. We regularly change leaders with votes, not guns or bloodshed. We have national, state, and local laws by which to live. And even if we don't like to obey them, we recognize how chaotic our society would be without them. We don't live under a tyranny of fear or the rule of the ruthless in our neighborhoods. Yes, living far from my homeland has helped me appreciate her even more.

BLESSED TO BE A BLESSING

My mind was consumed with the thought, *How blessed I am.* The word "blessing" doesn't get used very often in our society beyond spiritual circles. We're a nation blessed, in spite of the fact that most of us don't know what that even means. A person or nation is blessed when they receive a valuable benefit from God or another person for which they have done nothing. A blessing is not deserved or earned. It comes with one condition: Its greatest benefits aren't received until the blessing is passed on to someone else. Ironically, the more we give blessings away, the more they come back to us and become our own.

A phrase I learned in college has been proven true to me repeatedly in my lifetime: "We are blessed to be a blessing." America continues to make mistakes in the world, but her shameless generosity confounds the nations. One key to our nation's greatness has always been our willingness to share so much of it with others. In fact, God loves a cheerful giver and richly rewards those who practice his philosophy of life that teaches, "It is more blessed to give than to receive."

I have stacked, carried, and distributed a literal mountain of wheat in Afghanistan that was grown in my homeland. Much of it was simply given to those in need. The overflowing piles that demonstrate the abundant blessings of our nation have humbled me. I can't remember that we ever had a shortage of food due to the fact that it wasn't available. Sometimes war and mud make delivery difficult, but the supply is always waiting somewhere.

The will to give to others, to help, is one of the beautiful core traits of our nation. I have been fortunate to be "at the fingertips" of that giving in places like Afghanistan. It has been an honor, privilege, and blessing for me. I trust that, between the lines of my stories, you have been able to hear the sincere gratitude of my Afghan friends, who freely receive these boundless blessings that America so freely gives. And I, too, join them in giving thanks to God. Perhaps our calling as a country is to bless God and be a blessing to others.

PRICELESS PRIVILEGE

When I was home for Christmas 2001 and the 2002 New Year, I was asked to speak on numerous occasions in a variety of settings, from TV studios to tiny round tables. People began to kid me that I couldn't utter a sentence without using the word "privilege."

Privilege—the joy of participating or experiencing something unique or uncommon. That perfectly describes how I feel. The word *privilege* shares with the word *blessing* the characteristic of being undeserved. I feel privileged to be alive, to be an American, to experience God's love, to have a Bible, to know Jesus the Savior, and to be able to serve the lovely people of Afghanistan.

I've learned that privileges don't usually come easily. Sometimes we find ourselves in places where we are privileged to give everything we have to causes greater than we are. I have been privileged to live in a certain place in a certain time.

Others, like thousands of war veterans, the firemen and policemen doing their duty at Ground Zero, the brave-hearted people who brought down the plane in Pennsylvania, the men and women who died in the Pentagon and the World Trade Center, soldiers who have given their lives inside Afghanistan, and many others have had the costly privilege of dying so that we might live with a new understanding of the value of life and liberty. The depth of its effect on our lives will measure the value of their sacrifice. Such privileges, either defending freedom or enjoying it, should be treasured as priceless gifts worth more than all the gold in Fort Knox.

EVIL BOWS BEFORE GOOD

During my December visit, I found my mind pondering the evil of 9/11. I read everything I could find on the events of the day. I memorized the words of Mayor Giuliani: "We have met the worst of humanity with the best of humanity." Countless Americans responded to the attacks with an undaunted determination and single-mindedness. They will not be undone by the voices or actions of the few, who turn to hatred or mindless retaliation. They don't get sidetracked by thinking that, if we had only been properly prepared ourselves, we could have stopped that wicked day from dawning. They are too busy on their own mission of mercy.

Only in the great land that we call America could Ground Zero cleanup endure for so long and be as thorough as it was. I have observed that countries and people involved with terrorism tend to dismiss tragedy as fate. They let evil overcome and twist them, instead of conquering evil with good. They would not have had the strength or stamina, compassion or concern to clean up the mess.

American citizens of every background and perspective not only worked hard to carefully remove the rubble and recover the victims; they were untiring in performing other random acts of kindness. Americans lined up for blocks to donate blood for the injured and dying. Contributed food, clothes, money, and so much more have mounted through the months to help the families of victims. I have been continually amazed that, in spite of the horrible aspects of the tragedy, so much triumph has come from the events of 9/11.

SOMETIMES SUFFERING

When the coalition forces, as instruments of justice, smashed the Taliban and Al Qaeda, one of my continual concerns was for the only other two Americans that were inside Afghanistan. Along with six other international workers and sixteen local Afghans, they had been paraded before the world as examples of what the Taliban would do to anyone who dared to differ with them in any way. Twenty-four people were scheduled for execution for their association with Christianity. All of them were being held in Kabul and were suffering in small jail cells. I couldn't help but wonder if the retreating Taliban might decide to harm their prisoners out of rage and retaliation.

What a moving moment to hear the radio announcement: "They are all free, unharmed." I cheered and cried. I thanked God, full of praise and gladness. Now they are all telling their story of God's daily mercy and gracious deliverance. Truly they persevered as prisoners of hope, who were being punished for their good deeds, only to have greater good come from it.

Jesus Christ taught that suffering and persecution may come to those who obediently follow him. Bad things can happen even to people doing good, because this world is full of darkness and evil. In fact, darkness hates light, and good rubs those who are evil the wrong way. Those who practice this selfish lifestyle further suppress the truth and avoid owning up to their own wickedness.

This truth about life should not surprise us. In fact, there is Someone who knows all about the pain of suffering unjustly. In fact, he is the only one who is respected by all world religions, portrayed as perfect, shown as sinless, characterized by miraculous power, and viewed as the ultimate doer of good. Yet we know how he was treated by the people of his day. Blinded by their traditions and tyranny, they executed Jesus Christ in an act of purely selfish evil. They murdered the very one who came to serve them and be a blessing to them.

However, the story is not one of defeat. The greatest tragedy the world has ever seen ended in the grandest triumph we will ever know. Jesus Christ was killed and laid in a tomb on Friday, but then on Sunday morning he arose from death. He arose! And in that incredible moment, he conquered Satan and sin, death and darkness, and the tyranny of terrorism in our world forever. Will evil win a few battles here on earth? Yes, it will. But the war has already been won. Jesus Christ is alive today and offers us the gift of life, eternal life. Truly the God of love has overcome evil with good.

Even though many people in our country don't embrace the grace and sufferings of Christ Jesus, they live and prosper under the American way—a system that has been greatly shaped by his teachings. Those who attempt to eliminate the Judeo-Christian influence in our society find that they have very little society left when they are finished.

Our country's character enables us to be democratic, to promote peace, to rally for righteousness, and to counteract the evil in our world through acts of compassion and missions of mercy. Our nation doesn't claim sole ownership to these traits. We're happy to share them, knowing they were first shared with us. We long to see as many people as possible worldwide living under societal systems that promote genuine goodwill, a love for life, and liberty for all.

I have now returned to Afghanistan, not only proud of the way my country has led the struggle to liberate the land in which I serve but also deeply proud of the way my countrymen have been an example of goodness to the world.

Hope Lives!

FEYZABAD, AFGHANISTAN—During my initial visit to Afghanistan in September of 2000, I expected to lay the ground-work for an adult educational institute in Feyzabad. That project combined my deep desire to teach with my longing to fill the gaps and meet the needs of people. However, circumstances dictated a divine detour. Nevertheless, during 2001, when conditions stabilized somewhat in Nowabad, I jumped at opportunities to push forward plans for the institute.

In June 2001, Seth, our program officer in Badakhshan, and I met for a coordination meeting in Feyzabad. Most of our relief efforts were winding down, or at least running smoothly. I asked Seth, in passing, if he had located any places suitable for setting up the institute. Sadly, he had been too busy to look. I knew the feeling. The few people he had asked about prime property just shook their heads. We prayed briefly and asked God to move this project ahead on his timetable.

The next day one of our supervisors mentioned a place that had just come up for rent. We went to check it out. Seth and I had already decided that our rent budget could not exceed one hundred twenty dollars per month. We were dreaming of a place that had at least eight rooms and space enough to build four latrines. We assumed that any compound we found would not have sufficient toilet facilities for students.

We walked about ten minutes from our Shelter for Life (SFL) office, following the directions we had been given. The landlord, Hajji Jon, met us at the gate. As we entered the compound yard, I was immediately impressed by the profusion of flowers and fruit trees. *A slice of paradise,* I thought. The scenery was beautiful, and it was in a peaceful location near the river in a secure neighborhood. It would be quite suitable for a postsecondary educational endeavor. The two-story building in the compound actually looked like a school or small college building. We knew we were at the right place at the right time.

We walked through the rooms, all eight of them. The place was perfect, we concluded. We could see the wonder in each other's grins, knowing that God was indeed providing for us. Now it was time to negotiate.

The landlord was an older fellow, who seemed very supportive of our plan to use his property as an educational institute. We used the Afghan negotiating technique of talking about some of the liabilities of the property. Some walls were cracking, and the paint had served its time. Several windowpanes were missing. The rustic electrical wiring that was dangling in a few rooms looked more dangerous than useful. We also reminded Hajji of our planned renovations, like the latrines and upgrading of some of the rooms.

All of this was the traditional Afghan approach that put things into the proper context of our intended purpose and how it would greatly increase the value of his property.

We finally asked, "How much is the rent?"

I had expected to haggle a little. We only had a one-hundred-twenty-dollar budget to put on the bargaining table.

His reply was exactly what we wanted to hear: "How about a hundred dollars a month?"

This truly was a fair price; a financially comfortable Afghan family couldn't pay more than that. We asked for a year's contract and continued to explain our ideas for the property, both our remodeling plans and the intended uses by the institute. He agreed to everything. And we left there with our much-desired contract in hand.

EDUCATIONAL ENDEAVOR

Over the next ten months, the project moved forward in several phases, in spite of the challenges of world events.

Phase 1: God gave us some private donations from DARE in the UK for the beginning renovation phase. We painted the school, carpeted it, put in windows, and beautified it with other basic necessities. The rooms were equipped with tables and teaching tools. We also had some of our engineers construct four latrines.

Phase 2: With the help of Professionals International, we offered some summer English classes in July 2001 to both men and women. That educational opportunity was well received by the local community. Our students included recent graduates of high school, students from the medical university, and some young educators, who wanted to improve their English language and teaching skills.

Phase 3: We received full funding from the Institute for Cultural Research (ICR) based in the UK, a connection originally facilitated by our friend Saira Shah and CNN. We entered this partnership at the end of 2001. Our agreement allowed us to get everything ready to open the institute for full operation in the spring of 2002.

Phase 4: We finished renovating the school. Among the stunning upgrades we were able to make was a laboratory equipped with twelve laptop computers. These were bought in the States, and I had the delightful duty of carrying them from Washington all the way into Feyzabad after Christmas. Thankfully, they all survived the trip (and my handling) unscathed.

Seth, our computer specialist, busied himself for several days networking them together. He wired up our solar system and a battery bank to power the PCs. *Voilá,* we had the first wireless, networked, computer lab in all of Afghanistan. Users are even able to send and receive e-mail through our Iridium satellite phones.

The million-dollar setups of the World Bank and other UN agencies in Kabul have already surpassed us, but our little institute is still one of a kind in a land that is scrambling to catch up with the twenty-first century.

Phase 5: The Feyzabad Vocational Institute officially opened in April 2002. Now fully functioning, we have English, computer, and health education courses for both men and women. Our vision is to empower local Afghans so that they can develop their own country by teaching and training others. We believe this project is a great success story that will provide education in a way that spreads from families to communities to schools to villages, and only God knows how much further. I am seeing my original hope of teaching and serving inside Afghanistan fulfilled in ways far beyond my wildest dreams.

UNEXPECTED CHALLENGES

KESHEM—Defeat of the Taliban certainly did not instantly end Afghanistan's woes. Early in the spring of 2002, another disaster struck northern Afghanistan. Massive earthquakes rocked the provinces of Badakhshan and Baghlan. These sobering quakes hit around the district of Keshem the first week of March. This area is about twenty-five miles south of Rostaq, on the northern shoulders of the Hindu Kush range.

One of the fascinating facts that wasn't reported in the first news bites about the earthquake was that Shelter for Life had begun working in that area a month before the tremors began. We were already there when we were needed "to respond quickly and compassionately." We're now inside the province of Baghlan, helping to rebuild the lives of those affected there. Targeting the area of Nahrin, we hope to live up to our name and provide shelter for life. Our staff is now constructing five thousand houses there.

Keshem first came to my attention when the WFP did a survey

to assess the impact of the drought. Keshem represented a rain-fed area where they wanted to allocate 2,232 metric tons of wheat. In WFP terminology, "rain-fed area" refers to places that are unable to irrigate crops. These poor villagers were dependent on the heavens for rain. But for whatever reasons, the skies were shut tight.

The farmers in these mountainous villages had no rivers or natural reservoirs to tap during the devastating drought. The Keshem region includes an estimated ninety thousand people and some seventy-five identifiable villages, many of whom fit the rain-fed profile. The wheat was to help compensate them for the great losses they suffered because of their parched land. WFP proposed a program that would run for nine months, until the next expected harvest.

This food program allotment was to support "community projects that the local people would do at their own initiative." The NGO was to coordinate with the local "Shura" (body of elders or village leaders) and help them carry out the locally led projects that they wanted to do. The NGO would provide materials, supplies, supervision, monitoring, training, resources, funds, and all the necessary reporting.

WFP would give the wheat as requested by the NGO, who would distribute it to all those who participated in community projects. A percentage (up to 10 percent) could be given free to nonworking beneficiaries, like widows, young orphans, elderly, or disabled persons. The rest of the workers would receive fifty kilograms of wheat for each ten days they worked. Whichever NGO accepted this task had to distribute at least 238 metric tons of wheat every month for nine months. This would mean keeping a workforce of over four thousand people busy every month.

In order to implement this massive mission and meet the desperate need in Keshem, WFP faced several significant problems. Like all the generous people in America, who have resources to give but no way to get them into the hands of the poor in

Afghanistan, WFP had no official partner to whom they could delegate this program. There were no international NGOs in Keshem with the capacity, budget, or personnel to pull off such a large project. The only two small NGOs there were already busy and stretched to capacity with important agricultural projects. WFP needed a partner to supervise the projects and handle the distributions. Other problems involved the inaccessibility of some of the villages. Some had no roads, while others could be reached only by trails that were too narrow or too dangerous for vehicle travel.

There were legitimate reasons why no international NGO was active in the Keshem area. Local warlords kept the region in severe turmoil. Keshem was divided between an upper area and a lower area. The upper area was under the hand of Hajji ("one who goes on pilgrimage to Mecca") Alrong. He was part of Rabbani's government. Mowmin Safar, one of Hekmatyar's cohorts, controlled the lower area. These two leaders were archenemies who had actually fought against each other many times. Their relationship offers a good example of the internal ethnic and power tensions that exist inside Afghanistan.

I actually had Afghan people warn me, "John, be careful in Keshem." When I asked why, I usually heard about the dangers of Mowmin Safar, who was known to kill his enemies in public to make a statement to the people. Friends also reminded me that Keshem is one of the "most Islamic" or "ferociously fundamental" areas in northern Afghanistan.

Hajji Alrong turned out to be an invaluable implementer and active ally. He is an honest man who loves to help us. In fact, he was one of the only local commanders that WFP partnered with directly. Usually, WFP partnered with an NGO for project implementation, but in Keshem, they gave a road project to Hajji Alrong before we arrived. They were right. He was doing an excellent work. He soon became a key player in our own food program and emergency response after the March earthquake.

We learned later that when WFP was discussing Keshem, someone in the meeting quickly said, "Contact Shelter for Life. They'll go there. They'll go anywhere." Apparently, our reputation as a pioneering agency led us to another new adventure but also an awesome opportunity to serve some of the poorest of the poor. We do aim to go where no one else goes or wants to go.

I signed the agreement with WFP in February 2002 and rose to meet this unexpected challenge. My first task was to meet Hajji Alrong. He was one of the most gracious, generous, good-hearted men I have met in Afghanistan. I spent several days at his house in Farman Quli. He has since become a good friend. We trust each other and work well together.

I was impressed at Hajji's roadwork, supervising skills, and the crew he already had laboring every day. Their hard work was making a marked improvement in their communities. SFL only came in to help them go even further with the work they wanted to do. We extended the projects and expanded the programs he had initiated. Soon, we had around three thousand men working every month.

EMERGENCY ASSISTANCE

Then the earthquake struck in early March. Because we were already in Keshem, we were able to respond quickly and compassionately. Thankfully, the mountains trembled and the earth shook during the day, so no one was killed. Everyone was awake and had a few seconds to exit their tottering homes before the roofs caved in. We pulled together various food items (wheat, cooking oil, beans, sugar) and nonfood items (tents, blankets, clothes, and kitchen sets) to give to the affected families. This was some of first assistance that reached many of those high-altitude, mountainous villages.

As with all our disaster responses, we conducted a survey to accurately assess the needs. Again, people were either amazed that I could speak Dari or didn't even notice that I was a foreigner. Our quick visits covered the greater-impact area, which included about twenty villages. We found that around two thousand families had been affected in some way.

We prioritized the survey and began within days after the earthquake to distribute supplies to the most vulnerable people. Our timely aid was enough to empower them to get on with their daily activities. Afghans are hardy people. They appreciated the help after the tremors but were anxious to get back to the business of living. We were happy to help them do just that.

EAGERLY EXPANDING

We are reconstructing 113 kilometers of road in Keshem, renovating a school and clinic, helping with water projects, and rebuilding irrigation systems. As of summer 2002, our expanded program now employs over seven thousand people each month. These activities involve added challenges, because they are constructed in the mountains. We're having to blast or dynamite in many areas. Local people are also building seven bridges so that travelers will be able to go where no one's driven before. We're providing engineering expertise, special supervised assistance, and a variety of supplies for implementing these community initiatives.

I had the privilege of riding the first vehicle to some now-drivable destinations. One trip is etched in my mind. As our Hilax truck reached the area of Katabola, the people began cheering and throwing candy on our car. This traditional Afghan practice occurs when someone buys a new possession, starts a new venture, or brings home a new child. Friends and neighbors shower or give candy as a sign of blessing and gratitude, usually coupled with a prayer. On this day they were thanking God for the new road and the arrival of the first vehicle. Many were openly wondering what this would mean for their futures. A genuine sense of hope rose in the air that day. And my heart was rejoicing as well.

Meanwhile we have looked for other ways to help Keshem develop her communities. I remember a joyous day when we were able to give some leftover emergency tents to two local schools. Twelve tents became extra classrooms at the boys' school because an additional three hundred students signed up this year. Eight tents expanded the capacity of the girls' school to handle an increase of 170 girls who were eager to learn. What a pure pleasure to provide a place for students to sit and learn how to read and write.

WARLORDS WORKING TOGETHER

Once our Keshem projects got underway, we set up a little local office and distribution center. I remember being in a meeting there one day with Hajji Alrong, reviewing the road projects. Hajji is a small man, but his facial features remind me of General Massoud. Very energetic and charismatic, he laughs readily with his *pakul* hat tilted back on his forehead. He persuades by peaceful friendship. He also wears his Muslim faith with genuine dedication. He seems sincere and appears to really care for people.

During our discussion, Mowmin Safar walked into the room. We had only met briefly before. Frankly, Mowmin looks mean. A long, scraggly beard covers a mouth that doesn't smile or laugh much. He persuades by intimidation and force. And he always has several soldiers with him as personal bodyguards.

Hajji and Mowmin silently stood face to face that day. I instantly remembered that these two men were supposed to be hated rivals. I quickly stood and greeted Mowmin formally. It was my duty as host and as a younger man.

Open hand to my breast, right hand extended, I said, *"Salaam Alekum."*

As he turned to me, his eyes softened a little. He returned the greeting and then offered the same words and gesture to Hajji.

Two Muslims, who don't always see eye to eye, shook hands that day under the roof of Keshem's only foreigner. These two warlords now work together as the main managers of our program in Keshem. The beauty of it all is that the three of us are building a friendship.

In an area of nearly ninety thousand people, I sometimes feel overwhelmed as the only American or outsider. But that day, I couldn't help but wonder, *Maybe I am here "for such a time as this" to be a peacemaker.* What a priceless privilege to join God in this role of rebuilding and reconciliation.

THE MISSION CONTINUES...

Our mission of mercy goes steadily on day by day. In many ways, we have only just begun. No one knows when it will conclude. Our hope is to faithfully serve the war-torn people of Afghanistan for as long as we are needed. We have come to understand that, in this complex world that is devastated by war, drought, and other disasters, there are no quick fixes. While it only takes seconds to completely obliterate a life, the reverse process of reconstruction may require a lifetime.

It's all about life. In fact, that's why we now refer to ourselves as Shelter for Life. Life is a precious gift from God. Life deserves a chance. Life is worthy of breathing, receiving an education, working, and tasting the hopes and dreams of divine destiny. Maybe this is what is meant by the words of Jesus Christ, who said, "The thief does not come except to steal, and to kill, and to destroy. I have come that they may have life, and that they may have it more abundantly" (John 10:10). And it seems to me that Afghanistan is the perfect place to put his words into action, for she has been fighting for her life for years.

We will continue to focus on rebuilding-life issues, because we know this results in reigniting hopes, refueling dreams, restarting relationships, and regaining joy and purpose for life. This is how we plan to utilize our staff, as well as our time, energy, and resources. Rebuilding the lives of those who have been wounded by almost every form of destruction, we believe, is a worthy endeavor. Hopefully, our continuing demonstration of the compassion and love of God, our Father, will draw people heavenward.

In this new era of freedom in Afghanistan, with a new resolve in our hearts, and with a new name—Shelter for Life International— we plan to passionately pursue what we believe we are divinely called to do: "Provide the poor wanderer with shelter" (Isaiah 58:7 NIV). And as long as God gives me life, I hope to serve him where I have come to feel completely at home . . . inside Afghanistan.

Maps of Afghanistan

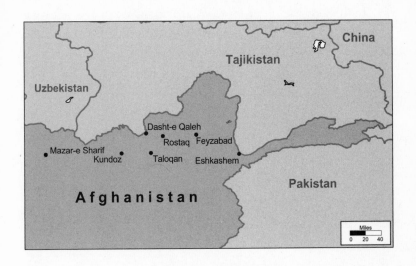

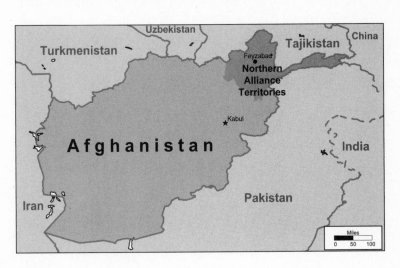

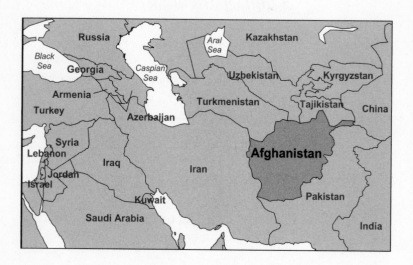

Contact Information

Would you like to know more about our work in Central Asia?
Perhaps even get involved in some way?
We would love to hear from you!
Together we can truly make the world
a better place as we share God's love
by compassionately serving others.

Contact:
DARE WORLDWIDE
P. O. Box 352
Turnbridge Wells
Kent, TN2 5XF
England
Telephone: +44(0)1892 531357
E-mail: D.A.R.E.@bigfoot.com

Shelter for Life International
P. O. Box 1306
Oshkosh, WI 54903
Surf: www.shelter.org

John Weaver
P. O. Box 271
Coats, NC 27521
E-mail: jmw3af@yahoo.com